THE
INSIDE GUIDE TO
FUNDING
REAL ESTATE
INVESTMENTS

ROSS HAMILTON

THE
INSIDE GUIDE TO
FUNDING
REAL ESTATE
INVESTMENTS

How to Get the Money You Need for the Property You Want

AMACOM

AMERICAN MANAGEMENT ASSOCIATION

New York • Atlanta • Brussels • Chicago • Mexico City • San Francisco
Shanghai • Tokyo • Toronto • Washington, DC

Bulk discounts available. For details visit:
www.amacombooks.org/go/specialsales
Or contact special sales:
Phone: 800-250-5308
E-mail: specialsls@amanet.org
View all the AMACOM titles at: www.amacombooks.org
American Management Association: www.amanet.org

This publication is designed to provide accurate and authoritative information in regard to the subject matter covered. It is sold with the understanding that the publisher is not engaged in rendering legal, accounting, or other professional service. If legal advice or other expert assistance is required, the services of a competent professional person should be sought.

Library of Congress Cataloging-in-Publication Data

Names: Hamilton, Ross, 1982- author.
Title: The inside guide to funding real estate investments : how to get the
    money you need for the property you want / by Ross Hamilton.
Description: New York, NY : AMACOM, 2017. | Includes index.
Identifiers: LCCN 2017007099 (print) | LCCN 2017024095 (ebook) | ISBN
9780814438862 (E-book) | ISBN 9780814438855 (pbk.)
Subjects: LCSH: Real estate investment.
Classification: LCC HD1382.5 (ebook) | LCC HD1382.5 .H355 2017 (print) | DDC
332.63/24--dc23
LC record available at https://lccn.loc.gov/2017007099

About AMA
American Management Association (www.amanet.org) is a world leader in talent development, advancing the skills of individuals to drive business success. Our mission is to support the goals of individuals and organizations through a complete range of products and services, including classroom and virtual seminars, webcasts, webinars, podcasts, conferences, corporate and government solutions, business books, and research. AMA's approach to improving performance combines experiential learning—learning through doing—with opportunities for ongoing professional growth at every step of one's career journey.

10 9 8 7 6 5 4 3 2 1

CONTENTS

FOREWORD

would like to take a moment to tell you a quick story about a broke, confused, injured person who couldn't even afford to buy a book. That person is me.

Well over a decade ago, I was a promising BMX rider. I spent nearly every waking moment at the skate park perfecting my stunts. I spent my days training with Dave Mirra and Ryan Nyquist (The Michael Jordans of the BMX industry) Then one day I suffered a career-ending injury. I had to come to the realization I was not going to be an X Games gold medalist and I had to craft a new plan.

I couldn't work while I was recovering so my small savings was dwindling very fast. I went to Barnes and Noble and stumbled across a book about real estate investing in the finance section. I couldn't afford to buy the $19 book, so every day I would go to the bookstore and pick up where I left off the previous day.

I read one statistic that motivated me and I will never forget it. More than 80 percent of millionaires are made through real estate. My perception of the entire world changed. I never checked the validity of that statistic, but it made sense that if I wanted to create real wealth, I needed to play the odds and get into real estate. Since then real estate has made me a millionaire many times over. But it all started when I picked up that first book. To find myself in your hands now is an honor and as a washed up broken BMX rider, I never imagined this moment.

I hope this is that book for you. That book that gives you a new perspective on life and what it *can be*. I hope it's that book that motivates you to take serious action. Why did I decide to write a book on the finance side of real estate investing? I've found most people believe they can't be a real estate investor because they don't have any money. Nothing can be further from the truth and this book will put that in focus for you.

I would like to dedicate this book to the people who've had the biggest influence in helping me reach financial heights that not too long ago seemed so far away.

First, to Napoleon Hill, the author of *Think and Grow Rich*. Although Mr. Hill and I never met personally, I have studied him extensively and feel like I know him well. His life's work has been the fuel that keeps me moving with a positive mental attitude through life's curve balls. The principles of successes discovered through Mr. Hill's work gave me a solid foundation to build my fortune on and it continues to inspire me today.

Second, I would like to dedicate this book to Doug Lebda, the founder and CEO of Lending Tree. His selflessness in sharing his life-changing wisdom has massively influenced my life, success, and abundance.

I also want to dedicate this book to all the men and women throughout the years who have spent time sharing their wisdom, connections, and resources with me. This includes the founders and fellow entrepreneurs I've met through Tek Mountain, the members of my Mastermind team, and most important the ConnectedInvestors.com team. A special thanks to a few team members: Bill Brinkley for helping me build an empire and Penny Myers for helping me make this book a reality.

This dedication is my way of recognizing all the people who have made such a big difference in my life. I am hoping that through this book I can serve you in the same way so many people have served me. This book is designed to give you a foundation to build your empire on and provide you with the wisdom, connections, and resources to help you reach your goals. No matter how big or lofty your goals may seem, in today's fast-moving, hyper-connected world, you are just a few moves away from life-changing success.

—ROSS HAMILTON
Founder and CEO of ConnectedInvestors.com

INTRODUCTION

People get involved in real estate investing for a variety of reasons. For most, the motivator is financial gain whether it be through short- or long-term strategies, tax advantages, or any number of other underlying reasons.

There are a lot of different ways to make money in real estate investment—it's the investor's personal choice which "investment vehicle" to choose. Will it be residential properties, commercial properties, or something like land banking? It's also a personal choice when it comes to investment strategy. Will it be fixing and flipping, renting homes or commercial property, or perhaps building new homes or commercial properties?

Regardless of the vehicle, the investor, or the strategy, there exists a set of common problems inherent in every real estate deal. Perhaps surprisingly, all real estate transactions follow a similar pattern. The common problems all investors face follow a pattern that goes something like this:

Find It. Not every property is a great choice for executing an investment strategy. Finding the really great deals, especially if you are a fix and flip investor, requires tenacity and resourcefulness. The same holds true for cash flow properties that are held for the mid- and long-term horizons. Not every house or every commercial property has the making of a great addition to a rental portfolio. Discovering the properties is the first step; the next step is the due diligence. Is the property truly profitable, and what warts does it come with?

Figure It. Once a potential investment property is discovered, the truth lies in the numbers and thorough due diligence. What problems need fixing? Are there title or other legal issues? Once your due diligence uncovers potential problems, the next question becomes can it make money as a fix and flip? You must have good information, accurate numbers, and the right formulas to figure that out. Is a property positioned to be a cash cow, providing monthly income and long-term benefits when held as a rental property? Again, due diligence and running the numbers are the key to sound decision making. Trip up here and there's potential for short- and long-term losses. Once a winner is uncovered, the next most common issue that investors face is funding the property and/or project.

Fund It. After due diligence is completed, the numbers are in, and formulas figured, it's time to determine the right kind of funding strategy for the property to meet the end goal. There are a variety of types of funding available for completely different purposes. Once the funding is in place, then you get to put the property to work as a fix and flip project, or perhaps a rental, or a development strategy.

Fix It. Rarely does an investment property change hands without some need for renovations or repositioning of some sort. Properties that are acquired at a great deal typically have more "potential" that needs to be realized. Usually the more warts a property has, the better the deal. For the fix and flip investor, this is where the money is made. But here's where there's an inherent problem. Most lenders don't want to make loans on rundown properties in need of repairs or rental properties that aren't performing. This book is designed to help you overcome the Fund It problem when there's a need to Fix It.

Flip It. If you've been involved at all in real estate investing, you may have heard the saying, "You make your money when you buy, not when you sell." The premise here is that the right purchase price has a huge impact on your overall profits. Fix and flip investors can't rely on appreciation in the market since their holding times are short. And hoping that your renovation comes in under budget is a fool's game. Successfully flipping properties is a numbers game, and the funding underlying the project can be a make-or-break proposition. Mismatched terms or rates that the property can't support are a recipe for disaster. A great buy on a piece of real estate can be undermined by bad financing.

Real estate investors at any point in the journey, from finding a great investment property to cashing in on its potential, run into roadblocks. Most are obstacles that can be overcome, but funding is most often the "stop you in your tracks" roadblock.

This book is designed to assist real estate investors with navigating the road to effective funding—especially funding for short-term projects like fix and flip properties or buy and hold strategies with a need for immediate, shorter-term acquisition funding. It also includes valuable information on traditional funding, crowdfunding, and working with individual private money lenders to help real estate investors find the best funding for their particular property or project.

Chapter 1 begins with a broad overview of real estate investing, to help you understand the myriad of real estate investment opportunities out there. Chapter 2 is a big-picture look at the types of real estate investment funding available in the current market. From there, I walk you through the finer points of each type of real estate investment funding with a definite focus on working with asset-based lenders who specialize in real estate investment capital.

While I wrote this book with the residential property investor in mind, many of the concepts included here apply to commercial investing as well.

THE BIG PICTURE
OF REAL ESTATE INVESTING

For many, the concept of "real estate investor" conjures up images of a skyscraper-owning mega-developer. For others, the image of real estate investor comes from those so-called reality shows about house flipping, where tens of thousands of dollars are made in a few short simple weeks of renovations. Neither of these offer an accurate representation of the real-world investor: The reality is a mash-up of people from all backgrounds, levels of experience, and income.

The Vehicle and Strategy

People get started in real estate investing typically because they have a desire to make money and create a lifestyle—and it can be done with great results. Real estate investors come in all varieties: Yes, there are skyscraper developers and there are house flippers making fortunes, but there are also average landlords cashing rent checks every month. There are mom-and-pop house flippers and there are real estate wholesalers crafting deals to pass along to other investors.

The things that distinguish them from each other are the investment vehicle and the exit strategy used to realize profits and create a lifestyle. It's important to know that aspiring investors don't need to have deep pockets or prior experience to invest in real estate. Certainly education and caution are warranted, but the barriers to entry may not be as challenging as many people think.

> The investment "vehicle" is the asset class a real estate investor chooses to invest in. Some choose residential properties such as single-family homes, multi-units, or apartment buildings. Others focus on commercial properties such as shopping centers, mini-storage facilities and warehouses, or industrial-use buildings.
>
> The investment "strategy" is the method used to reposition a property for profitability. Strategies are defined mostly by the "exit"—the technique used to realize profits. Our focus is on wholesaling, fixing and flipping, and buy and hold investments.

So, what makes an investor choose one investment vehicle or exit strategy over another? For the most part, it's any of three things: time, money, or skills. These three important factors impact not only the investment vehicle, but also the strategy.

Three Common Real Estate Investment Exit Strategies

1. **Wholesaling.** A wholesaler specializes in finding great deals on properties and passing those deals along to investor buyers for a fee. The buyer of wholesale properties is usually a fix and flip or buy and hold investor. Many people are exposed to wholesalers on a regular basis but don't realize it. When you see a WE BUY HOUSES sign, you are probably seeing the marketing efforts of a local wholesaler. The wholesaler acts as a middleman and earns a fee for finding the seller (i.e., the property), negotiating

the deal, and executing the contract. Once wholesalers have a property under contract, they find a capable investor buyer and use an assignment clause to transfer the right to purchase the property to the investor, who then fixes and flips it or keeps it as an income property.

2. **Fixing and Flipping.** Flippers, as they are often called, bring a distressed property up to market standards and resell it for profit. Fix and flip investors need to find great deals on properties that can be renovated and resold in a relatively short turnaround time. Flippers often rely on local wholesalers to locate properties with good profit potential.

3. **Buy and Hold.** Probably the most familiar investment strategy is buy and hold—commonly known as "landlording." Landlords purchase property for the express purpose of holding it to generate passive rental income and the potential for long-term gains through market appreciation.

With each of these strategies come unique needs in terms of time, money, and skills (see Table 1-1).

For anyone involved in real estate investing, it is helpful to consider the end goal as you approach each opportunity. Questions to ask include:

- How do the properties you are looking at fit into the big picture?
- What do you want the property to do for you in terms of short- or long-term gain?
- How does the property fit with your capacity to invest your time, money, and skills?

If you have a lot of money but not a lot of time, a buy and hold strategy could be your thing. If you have more time than money, wholesaling could be the ideal gig for you. It pays to really take a close look at the personal commitment that the different investing strategies require and determine if a strategy fits your ideals.

Table 1-1. **Three Common Real Estate Investment Strategies.**

Strategy	Money	Skills	Time
Wholesaling	Wholesalers are marketing machines: They're trying to find as many deals as possible as frequently as possible. Although wholesaling doesn't require funding per se, the wholesaler does need cash for marketing and finding motivated sellers.	Must be good at ferreting out good deals, negotiating with sellers (and kissing lots of frogs), and marketing deals to a buyer's list of cash investors.	Wholesaling can be done on a part-time basis but takes a good marketing system to be able to execute multiple deals each month. This is a wash-rinse-repeat business model.
Fix and Flip	House flipping requires short-term cash for the acquisition of the property and then plenty of cash for the renovations. Typically a flip is completed and sold within a six-month period—for some it will be more; for others it will be less. It's critical to plan your funding accordingly.	Must have solid market and end-buyer knowledge; a good team to execute the legal, construction, and marketing; and most important, the ability to assess and manage a home renovation.	Whether you are a DIYer or manage a crew, house flipping is a big time commitment, but the payoff can be excellent. Flipping houses is also a wash-rinse-repeat business model in order to keep cash flowing in.
Buy and Hold	The buy and hold investor/landlord needs access to long-term cash. While the wholesaler and flipper make chunks of cash on sales, the buy and hold investor is building wealth through rental income paydown of mortgages and long-term appreciation of the property.	Landlords first and foremost must have good tenant screening skills and procedures. They also need to be skilled at "running the numbers," making sure the property is generating cash flow and making adjustments as needed.	Landlording is considered "passive income," but any experienced landlord will tell you it's not passive. Turnovers, repairs, and other demands of owning rental real estate make it very much an active strategy—it just may not be daily activity.

More About Exit Strategies

Having clear exit strategies is critical for any investor in any niche. Every property should have a Plan A to take it toward profitability. Understanding how to apply strategies that target short-, mid-, and long-term goals will help to make determining your exits even easier. Experienced investors in all asset classes know that you have no business getting into an investment unless you've got a clear path out.

Consider the End Before Beginning

So what's the endgame you can consider right now, given your level of time, money, and skills?

For a buy and hold strategy, questions to ask include:

What's your monthly income going to look like?

How will you fund the acquisition of the property?

How long will you keep the property and why?

What will you do with the proceeds when you decide to sell?

For fixing and flipping, you need access to funds to get you where you want to go. If you don't have a clear exit strategy that demonstrates expected returns and timelines for repayment, don't expect an easy road to funding. Questions to consider:

How long until you can cash out?

What's the cost of your funding?

What's your expected profit?

What will you do with the proceeds?

Is this something you want to do again and again?

If you are wholesaling only:

How much in wholesale fees would you like to earn?

How many marketing leads do you need to make enough offers to close enough deals?

What market will you target?

What will you do with the money you make, and are you willing to wash, rinse, and repeat to keep the fees coming in?

A Path to Success

It's not uncommon for those new to real estate investing to start as a wholesaler and then progress toward both flipping and owning income properties. Wholesalers don't need cash to get started, but they do need to develop certain skills. As a successful wholesaler, you learn how to find great deals, assess property repairs and values, and negotiate contracts. These skills readily transfer to fix and flip investing. The smart wholesaler can learn the game and use earnings from wholesale fees to actively buy, fix, and flip properties for even more gain than is realized by wholesaling. Then, profits from fix and flip properties can provide lump sums to purchase rental properties that generate income more passively. Over time, the investor's time, money, and skills develop, allowing for the use of higher net profit strategies.

Chapter 18, "How to Land the Best Loans for Your Deals," covers the types of funding and loan features that can best facilitate your exit strategy and big-picture plan. Each investor and asset class has different needs when accessing capital for investment properties and projects. The next chapter more broadly covers the types of funding options available to investors.

🏠 TAKEAWAYS

- *Revisit Table 1-1's money, skills, and time requirements. When you think about these needs, which strategy will work for you right now, and why?*
- *Which strategy would you like to use five years from now, and how do you plan to get there?*

AN OVERVIEW
OF FUNDING OPTIONS

S ince the 2000s, real estate investment funding along with traditional mortgage lending have gone through significant changes. During the bubble years early in the decade, money for purchasing real estate was readily available. Lenders loosened up loan qualification criteria for homeowners and investors alike, and the end result was too many bad mortgages. This impacted the entire real estate market, and ultimately capital for purchasing real estate became difficult if not impossible to secure.

Fast-forward to the recovery of the real estate market and you find that the lending landscape has improved along with the market. The real estate investor who had been shut out of most borrowing opportunities now finds the capital for investment property purchases more readily available. Lenders realized that there is a huge appetite for funding investment properties. With the market flush with opportunities to purchase foreclosures and other types of distressed properties, lenders have responded by securing and loaning capital specifically for real estate investment.

Here, I want to introduce the four primary sources of funding for investment properties. In upcoming chapters, each is covered in more detail.

Traditional Mortgage Lending

This type of loan is familiar to most of us—it's the conventional mortgage underwritten to government Fannie Mae and Freddie Mac guidelines, most often used by homeowners. The loans are offered by banks and mortgage brokers. When financing an owner-occupied home, the traditional loan is the go-to source for purchase monies. During the bubble years, it was even possible for investors to source funds through traditional lenders. Of course, that all changed with the 2008 market crash. The fallout from that event is still felt by investors, who continue to be challenged by traditional lenders' underwriting criteria for down payments and loan-to-value and debt-to-income ratios, along with their reluctance to finance properties in need of significant repairs. Combine that with the extended time it takes to close a traditional loan and the result is a borrowing climate that often cannot meet the needs of real estate investors. Despite the challenges of securing traditional funding, it is still possible on rental-income-producing properties for the investor with verifiable income, great credit, and a big down payment to meet the rigors of underwriting.

Asset-Based Loans

Asset-based lenders for real estate investment are also known as hard money lenders. The term "hard money" is derived from the fact that the loan is secured by a hard asset; however, some people joke that hard money is "easy money with hard terms." It is easier to qualify for hard money loans, but it comes at a cost. Higher interest rates and shorter terms are the norm, and for many fix and flip investors in particular, the cost is justified by the profit potential. There are caveats, however, and those interested in hard money should pay careful attention to Chapters 12 and 13, which focus on hard money lenders and their terms. Some investors use hard money to acquire and renovate properties, and then seek traditional long-term funding to finance the property for rental purposes.

Private Money Loans

It's possible to borrow money for investment properties from private individuals. Private money loans are typically secured the same way as traditional and hard money loans. The property is used as collateral and repayment terms are outlined in legally executed loan documents. Private money has the distinct advantage of being the most flexible of all sources of funding. Whereas banks and hard money lenders set the rates and terms, when working with a private money lender, there's opportunity for negotiating rates and terms. Finding the individuals who can and will loan money for real estate is a process of relationship building, but once established, private money can be a go-to source for fast and flexible funding for both short- and long-term loans.

Crowdfunding

It is now possible for real estate investors to secure funding for real estate deals through crowdfunding. There are multiple ways to secure funding from "the crowd," with the property, the project, and the numbers dictating the best strategy. All crowdfunded property investments are listed and administered by third parties. They make the investment offering public through their web portal and manage all aspects of the financials and legal requirements. More often than not, crowdfunded properties are larger commercial projects like apartment buildings, shopping centers, and new developments that can benefit from financial repositioning of debt and equity. The market for crowdfunding smaller projects like fix and flip single-family homes is still in its infancy. If you are thinking of crowdfunding your deal, check out Chapter 7 for more about the use of crowdfunding to finance properties. It's also possible to invest in other people's properties via online crowdfunding portals. While you don't become a partner or owner in the property, you have the option to invest in debt or equity positions.

Chapter 8, "The New Kid on the Block: Crowdfunding," covers this option in more detail.

Funding for real estate investing is readily available—and not all borrowers need to have A+ credit and big down payments. Hard and private money make it possible to jumpstart a new real estate investor or keep the seasoned investor supplied with capital for properties and projects.

TAKEAWAYS

- *What did you discover about alternative types of funding that has the potential to boost your real estate investing capacity?*
- *How can you combine your "time, money, and skills" profile (Table 1-1) with alternative sources of funding to jumpstart your real estate investing activities?*

3

AN INTRODUCTION
TO ASSET-BASED LOANS

Is Asset-Based Lending What You Need?

Asset-based lending is expanding rapidly and real estate investors are now able to tap into this nearly unlimited supply of funding for their real estate deals. Funding can be secured through local lenders; even more convenient for today's investor, it can be done online with the click of a few buttons.

For anyone involved in real estate, it is very important to understand what asset-based lending is and how to find quality asset-based real estate lenders. Asset-based lending is a broad term that usually describes lending that is specifically used for business purposes. At its very core, asset-based lending is a business loan that is secured by some sort of asset as collateral. Assets can include a real property, business inventory, accounts receivable, or other balance sheet assets.

So, when something of value is pledged as collateral, it's an asset-based loan. But we're not talking about a traditional homeowner's loan that uses the home as collateral. We're talking about asset-based lending for *real estate investing*, which has its own set of rules, purposes, sources, and pluses and minuses. The most common types of asset-based loans for real estate investing are hard money loans and private money loans.

Hard money is readily available to investors, is typically offered by companies or private lenders, and comes with strict guidelines for everything from project plans to draws for paying contractors to repayment terms (usually very short).

Private money loans are issued by individuals and can be much more flexible, but you have to know who to ask. It can take months, even years, to develop a network of private money lenders to work with. Whether you use hard or private money loans, building a strong working relationship is the key to being able to go back for more project funding.

Real estate investors find asset-based lending attractive because loans are based on the property or project, rather than the personal credit history or cash position of the borrower. Instead, lenders look at the numbers and the exit strategy and anticipated return for the investor. They look at the as-is value of the property and the after-repair value of the property if it is a fix and flip. They look for safety in the numbers of the deal rather than debt-to-income ratios and credit scores of the borrower (as covered in great detail in other sections).

These loans work great for real estate investors since many are self-employed; some may have existing mortgages that exclude them from traditional bank financing that limits the number of loans an individual can secure. And for those new to investing, asset-based lenders offer funding options that a traditional lender might not. So, unlike the homeowner who has to prove income, existing debts, and a whole lot more, an investor looking for asset-based funding needs to document the viability of the property and its intended use and anticipated outcome.

There's been an explosion of asset-based lenders in recent years because there's a huge demand for investor financing. You know what they say—money follows opportunity, and lenders woke up to the fact that real estate investors have been cut out of the traditional lending model and there has been pent-up demand for funding real estate deals.

There's a yin and yang to everything, so here's what to be aware of when considering using asset-based loans, including hard money and private money loans.

The Good, the Bad, the Ugly, and the Facts of Working with Asset-Based Lenders

- Good: Getting funded is easier than working with a bank.
- Bad: Among asset-based lenders, 99 percent will require you put at least 5 percent down. Some will require more.
- Ugly: It's a lot more expensive than a bank.
- Fact: Funding can be acquired quickly.
- Fact: The borrower needs to document the project thoroughly.
- Fact: Repayment terms are short, typically 6 to 60 months.
- Fact: Loans must be in first position against the property.
- Fact: Loans are only given to investors buying property at deep discounts.
- Fact: Asset-based lenders understand real estate investors.

That covers the basics of asset-based loans for real estate investing. Subsequent chapters get into more specifics about when and how to use hard money loans, private money loans, and several other alternatives for funding real estate deals.

TAKEAWAYS

- *What's the main difference between a hard money loan and a private money loan?*
- *What do hard and private money lenders have in common?*

4

AN INTRODUCTION
TO HARD MONEY LENDERS

Can Hard Money Lenders Be a Good Source of Funding for You?

Hard money has been called easy money with hard terms: It may be fairly easy to borrow, but the lender's terms are hard and almost always include relatively high interest, even higher "origination" fees, a short payback period, and high monthly payments. Not all lenders are created equal, however, and you'll see wide variation in all of the terms and the qualifying criteria to secure the loan. Hard money is always secured by the asset (collateral)—and for the real estate investor, that collateral is the subject property.

> **$** There are two kinds of hard money lenders. Hard money brokers pool the funds of private money lenders and loan the funds to borrowers. They also manage the servicing of the loan. Then there are private money lenders who loan direct to borrowers without a hard money broker acting as a middleman. Both use similar terms and criteria for lending, but again, not all are created equal, and it's up to you to determine the best lender for your needs.

There are pros and cons to using hard money for your real estate investing, but the bottom line is, well . . . the bottom line. If the property and the project support the cost of the funds, then hard money borrowing can offer investors the opportunity to participate in deals they might not have otherwise. A common mantra: "Part of something is better than all of nothing."

Another plus with hard money loans: They are easier to access than traditional financing and can often be closed in a matter of days, not weeks and months as with a typical mortgage. Hard money loans aren't based on the borrower but rather the property and the exit strategy. Banks may lend at much lower rates, but their criteria are much more stringent. Banks evaluate you, the borrower, as their primary qualification. By contrast, hard money lenders evaluate the investment property as the primary qualification, which allows them to move more quickly and require much less documentation. Typically, the after-repair value of the property is used to evaluate your loan, something banks don't typically consider.

Who Uses Hard Money Loans?

- New real estate investors who can't demonstrate enough income or cash reserves for a bank to qualify them
- Investors with poor credit, undocumented income, or a short work history
- Experienced investors with more than four mortgages in their name
- Investors buying properties that need significant repairs
- Buyers who need renovation funding, not just purchase funds
- Investors who don't have the cash required to close with a conventional loan
- Real estate investors who are highly leveraged elsewhere
- Buyers of properties that won't appraise as-is for an acceptable value

- Buyers dealing with distressed sales that must close in days, not weeks
- Buyers of rental properties that are under-rented, in need of repair, or otherwise problematic
- Property owners with high equity who need quick access to cash for any reason

As you evaluate your deal and decide whether or not to use hard money, you have to consider a few key factors.

1. What's your intended exit strategy? If that doesn't work, what's your Plan B?
2. Does the property and exit strategy support the higher cost of hard money?
3. Can you document your exit plan, project plan, and capacity to profit?
4. Can you meet the deadlines imposed by the terms of the loan?

On the surface, it may seem like hard money isn't the best deal—but hard money can get you in the game when you may have been shut out otherwise. It meets the needs of a lot of different investors and borrowers despite the higher costs and shorter terms. The simple fact is that hard money has funded many successful fix and flips and other types of real estate–related projects.

Reliable access to funding can make or break even the best deal on real estate. Real estate investors often rely on nontraditional sources of funding for their short- and long-term projects for a couple of really good reasons: Traditional lenders are too slow to close, and time is of the essence in investment deals. This makes asset-based lenders such as hard money lenders a good and viable option.

TAKEAWAYS

- *List three big advantages of hard money loans:*
    1.
    2.
    3.
- *When would you consider using a hard money loan?*

5

WHAT YOU NEED TO KNOW
ABOUT PRIVATE MONEY LENDERS

Can Private Money Lenders Be the Answer for You?

As a real estate investor, you spend a lot of time researching target markets, generating leads, and finding the best deals that have the highest return on investment. Of course, you also have to fund those deals, and private money lenders are sometimes the best source to turn to when you want to buy an investment property.

Whether you are fixing and flipping properties or your plan is to fix and hold them, you can't achieve your goal without the right funding—and to get the right funding you must understand who private lenders are, how to find them, and what they want in return for lending you the cash to complete your investments. When you understand these factors, you'll be able to weigh the pros and cons and decide if you should go to a private money lender to fund your next property.

Who They Are

First of all, private money lenders are not banks. They may be individuals, or they may be small companies representing a number of private money lenders. In either case, they are willing to lend money to investors for real estate purchases that are not as easily funded through traditional banks and mortgage lenders.

Attempting to fund an investment property with a traditional mortgage can be more difficult than qualifying for a mortgage to buy your primary residence—even if you have great credit and assets. Traditional lenders have their niche—the "owner-occupant" homeowner—so getting a loan from them for any other purpose can be a big challenge.

As a result, there is tremendous demand out there for money for real estate investments. Private money lenders fulfill that demand by lending money through real estate–secured, asset-based loans. When you borrow from a private money lender you agree on a set interest rate and time that you will pay back your loan, which is much like working with a traditional lender. But with private money lenders, the rates are generally higher and loan periods shorter. The loan is secured by the property; if you don't make your payments on time, the property can be foreclosed and the lender takes possession and takes action to recoup—much like a traditional lender would.

Just like a hard money lender, a private money lender will focus more on the value of your property and its potential for returns, rather than qualifying you based on your income and/or net worth. But the smart private money lender will also look into the borrower's capacity to repay the debt.

Two Types of Private Money Lenders

Asset-Based Lending Companies (Including Hard Money Lenders)

The basics of hard money are covered in Chapter 4. But it's important to know that with the growth of real estate investing comes the need for more and better funding options. Asset-based lending companies are often made up of groups of private money lenders who specialize in funding investment properties and projects.

Private Money Lenders (Individuals)

Unlike hard money lenders, who focus almost solely on the collateral worth of your property and will typically charge a much higher interest rate, individual private money lending is very much a relationship-based business with fewer hard-and-fast rules. Unless you're working through a company that pools the funds of private money lenders, you'll work with an individual with funds available to loan.

It pays for investors to network and build relationships with potential private money lenders; when you are tapped into a personal network, you can close more deals because you have more access to capital.

When you work with private money lenders and show them that you can be trusted to pay their loans and bring them good returns for their money, you can expect that they'll want to do deal after deal.

For them, it's safe and easy returns. And for you, it's assurance that when a deal is in front of you, you can get the funding to close it. Many investors use the same private money lenders over and over because they've developed that kind of win-win relationship. The investor gets the deal funded and makes money, while the lender earns interest from a loan secured by hard assets—the property.

The local bank or the "too big to fail" bank is no longer willing to loan you investment capital in a post-bubble market. This puts hard and private money sources at the front of the line for real estate investors seeking funding.

Of course, to use private money lenders to finance your investments, you'll need to know how to find them. Unlike banks and hard money lenders, private money lenders don't advertise, but they may be closer to you than you think.

How to Find Private Money Lenders

Private money lenders are individuals who have the funds available to finance a real estate investment and, more important, would be willing to secure a loan on your property with the title or deed to your investment property in exchange for returns.

Many investors find private money lenders among their family, friends, and/or colleagues. And, as more and more individuals are disappointed with traditional investments, they are looking for these alternatives.

When considering who to approach, you may want to take two important things into consideration:

1. Is this potential private lender knowledgeable about real estate? When working with individuals who already know and understand real estate, you put yourself ahead of the game. It's certainly fine to work with novices in real estate—just expect to have to do more educating and even hand-holding throughout the process of funding and repaying the loan.

2. Does this person have personal knowledge of me, my business, and my track record?
   Again, those who already know you will be much easier to approach, but don't limit yourself to that network. It's pretty easy to "show your work" to a potential new private lender. Pull together some photos, some numbers, and a summary of a few select projects.

What Lenders Want

Perhaps we should start with what they don't want. Private money lenders don't want hassles, they don't want to foreclose, they don't want to own the property, and they don't want difficulties in earning their returns. Most private money lenders have no interest in being a "real estate investor"—they want to be a private lender who earns nice returns for the risk involved in funding your property. What they want is to earn easy returns for the risk of lending to you. That's the big picture of what they want, but here's the rubber-hits-the-road things your private lender will want from you before considering your funding request:

- **The Contract.** Most lenders want to see the contract you've executed to purchase the property.
- **Photographs.** If you are purchasing a fixer-upper, be ready to provide photos.
- **A Summary.** Put together a simple summary for your lender. Include the purchase price, the renovation costs, and the after-repair value (ARV) supported by comparables.
- Some lenders, especially if working with you for the first time, would appreciate a list of your "team." Who's your closing attorney? Your insurance agent? Your contractors?

Put yourself in the position of your lender and ask yourself, "If I were loaning someone $100,000, what would I need from them to make the decision to do so?" That tells you everything you need to have ready. And, of course, just ask them! Experienced private money lenders already know what they need—and you'll probably find that novice lenders want even more information.

The Importance of Relationships

Private money loans are more relationship-based than hard money loans—but make no mistake: Many investors have strong relationships with their hard money lenders and do repeat business because both the relationship and the numbers work.

No matter who it is, your lender wants you to succeed in your investment. For lenders, your property and project may be the fastest, safest, and most efficient way for them to make a profit by loaning you the funds. To ensure that they are making the right choice in loaning you money, they'll want to know about you, your current

investment, and your track record with real estate investments and/
or other lenders and investors. Never be shy about sharing your
successes!

Money follows opportunity, and the more your potential lenders
know about you and your investing niche, the more likely they'll be
to finance your investment. That's why it pays to network and build
relationships with private lenders. If you've chosen a good investment and you have a solid plan for it, it's a mutually beneficial deal
that both parties will likely want to repeat in the future.

The Benefits of Private Money

All of that sounds like a great deal, as long as you can find a lender
who meshes well with you and your investment(s) and who will
charge you a fair rate on your loan. As you approach funding your
deals, consider all the benefits of private money.

Pro: Ease of Qualification

First of all, when you work with a private money lender, you only
have to provide information that demonstrates that you've found a
good investment that will pay off and create a win-win for everyone.
You'll find there are far fewer hoops to jump through with a private
money lender than with a traditional mortgage lender.

While private money lenders typically don't charge interest rates
quite as high as hard money lenders, the rates are still higher than
you'd get from a bank. But it's kind of a moot point if you consider
that most investors can't get approved for a loan with the bank.

The math on your interest rate is simple. If the property and
the numbers support it, accessing the funding is worth it. Again,
"part of something is better than all of nothing"—so don't let the
higher cost of asset-based funding dissuade you when the numbers
work. Private lending allows you to get involved when you otherwise might not.

Pro: Geared Toward Investors

Private money lenders understand that you are purchasing, refinancing, and/or rehabilitating a property based on its after-repair value, not its current value. More often than not, they lend you all of the money you need to achieve your goals with your investment, which is another upside compared to what you might get with a traditional loan.

Pro: Fast Way to Get Money

This is huge. We know that purchasing investment real estate is very competitive. Time is of the essence, and the person who has the cash, wins! The so-called approval process is much shorter with private money lenders than it is with banks and mortgage lenders and even some hard money lenders. If you've landed a deal and have a property under contract, it's possible to get it funded within days instead of weeks or months. When you go with a private money lender, "time is of the essence" is less a burden and more of an easy call to action.

Private money lenders offer a lot of opportunities and advantages to real estate investors. While you may have to pay a higher interest rate, you can get funding quickly to rehab and then resell your property, so you'll see a return on your investment much faster than you could with most other financing options. You also have the opportunity to build relationships, create win-wins, and then do it all over again.

TAKEAWAYS

- *Describe your ideal private money lender.*
- *List potential lenders already in your network.*
- *List those in your network with real estate experience and those without any previous knowledge of real estate.*

6

HOW TO TAKE THE MYSTERY
OUT OF PRIVATE MONEY

Is It Really Possible to Borrow from
Private Individuals?

One of the biggest hang-ups new and even experienced investors have is centered on getting capital for their investments. We can't control the banks and their (un)willingness to lend on investment deals, but what we can do is tap into the billions of dollars in capital out there that's underutilized and getting measly returns.

So to get you past this concern, we're going to try to take the mystery out of using other people's money (OPM) to fund your buy-fix-sell deals. Too often when considering private money loans, investors who've never worked with a private money lender will get that blank stare that then spirals down into all sorts of objections.

- I don't know anyone with that kind of money . . .
- I don't know how to approach someone if I did . . .
- I have no idea what to offer a private money lender . . .
- I haven't got a clue how to structure a deal like that . . .
- I don't know what paperwork to do . . .

All of these "I don't knows" are rooted in a simple lack of experience and, let's be honest, fear.

So, let's set aside the fear of the unknowns and take some mystery out of borrowing from a private money lender and hopefully give you the confidence to finally ask for private funding.

> There's nothing inherently scary about borrowing from a private lender as opposed to an institution. The big difference is the institution tells you how it will work. When you work with a private money lender, you and your lender determine how it works . . . a big plus for you, the investor captaining the deal.

There are two primary things you must address when considering a private money loan.

First, you must understand how the money works for you and how it works for your lender. So you need to learn some basic terms to use when working up a privately funded real estate deal.

Second, you must understand the competition. By that I don't mean competition from other real estate investors, buyers, or sellers—I'm talking about the competition for your lender's dollars. Can you beat the prevailing returns that lenders are getting in their current investment vehicle? If so, you can capture the attention (and the business) of more than one private money lender.

The Components of a Private Money Loan

To help you understand how the money works, let's set up an example that shows the three basic components of a private money loan transaction.

1. **The Property.** In the case of a single-family home, for this example, we've identified an opportunity for a fix and flip property with the potential to net $40,000 or more after it sells. The purchase agreement is executed.

2. **The Mortgage.** This is the basic instrument that ties the property to the promissory note. It's your lender's security, and works to secure collateral (the asset) for the loan. The mortgage is recorded as public record and identifies the property, the borrower, the lender, and the dollar amount, along with the lender's recourse in case of default. It can be prepared by any qualified real estate closing attorney.

3. **The Note.** This is the IOU from you to your lender—the promissory note. This is not public record; it is the financial agreement between you and your lender that outlines your promise to pay, including the dollar amount, the terms such as interest, and the repayment periods—basically the when, where, and how you will repay the loan. The promissory note can also be prepared by a qualified real estate closing attorney.

A Sample Deal

Here's an example of how you can work with a private money lender. It could be Uncle Bob, a former coworker, your closing agent, just about anyone. Put your brain on it and you'll figure out who to ask. Plus, once you understand how private money works, you are going to be excited about offering the opportunity to make money together.

Let's say you find a property for $50,000 that could be renovated for $36,000 and resold. You'll need at least $86,000 to purchase and renovate the property. So, to close the deal, you'll need a private money loan for $86,000. You've determined that the property will net $128,000 after concessions and sales costs. With $86,000 in the deal, the net profit comes in at $42,000.

Identify those in your circle who have money (probably because they like to make money) and offer them the opportunity to make, for example, 12 percent interest on their money or 15 percent of the profit, whichever is greater.

In this example, if you buy, fix, and resell the property in six months, you're offering them something that looks like either of these scenarios:

Based on 12 Percent Interest

- $86,000 loan × 0.12 (annual interest rate) = $10,320. Since you're only borrowing the money for six months, adjust accordingly.
- $10,320/12 (months) = $860 × 6 (months) = $5,160 in earnings for your private lender.

Based on 15 Percent of Profit

- $42,000 profit × 0.15 = $6,300 in earnings for your private lender.

You don't have to be a math whiz or financial adviser to figure out that this is a great deal for your lenders. They are fixed at 12 percent interest to earn. But if the deal is even sweeter, they have the potential to earn even more with the 15 percent of the profit option. It's a win-win. You get the funds you need to fund your flips and they earn great returns on their dollars languishing in a CD or lazy IRA.

Now that you understand the mechanics of the money, let's revisit the paperwork, which we already touched on. It involves the property (i.e., the house and the contract to purchase it), the mortgage, and the promissory note.

Putting It on Paper

Once you have the property under contract, put together a summary of the house and project. Meet with your potential lender and outline the terms you can offer (yours may be higher or lower than in our example, but it's incumbent on you to determine what the property and project can support).

Discuss how the promissory note outlines the terms of the loan and repayment and also how the mortgage secures the note against the property. You may not need to have this discussion with some private money lenders—they already get it—but for those who don't, you must be prepared to explain it.

Once you come to an agreement on terms, contact your closing attorney to execute the legal documents.

This is a basic overview. The intent is simply to help you overcome the fear of the deal and understand that it's not all that complicated. Money follows opportunity—that's how it's made. With a better understanding of how to structure your deals and pay your private money lenders, you can approach more opportunities and ultimately have lenders seeking you out to do business.

TAKEAWAYS

- *Why would an individual want to loan you money for your deal? Think about this carefully. When you approach potential lenders, you have to be able to explain the advantages of loaning you money for your deal.*
- *Consider this example: You found a property that you could purchase for $40,000 that needs $25,000 in repairs that will net $110,000 when sold.*
    1. *What is your private lender's return if you borrow at 12 percent?*
    2. *What is your private lender's return if you offer 15 percent of the net profit?*

7

THINKING OF
CROWDFUNDING YOUR DEAL?

The Basics You Need to Know

For any number of reasons, a property or project may not be feasible for traditional lending. Crowdfunding real estate is increasingly becoming the tool of choice to fill the financial gap for the project's principals and developers.

Crowdfunding has exploded since the JOBS (Jumpstart Our Business Startups) Act of 2012 opened the door for accredited and now, finally, nonaccredited investors alike to participate. Initially, only high net worth "accredited" individuals could participate in crowdfunding, which effectively shut out the average investor. Regulations opened the door for nearly anyone to get involved, and today you see more crowdfunded properties available for investment opportunities than ever before. All of these changes create an environment where online crowdfunding platforms can serve as a solid solution for the future of real estate investing and redevelopment.

The Basic Model

The basic crowdfunding model includes three primary entities:

1. **The Project (the Investment Sponsors/Developers).** People and organizations propose the projects to be funded. They are seeking funding from the next entity.

2. **The People (the Investors).** They are, in essence, "the crowd" who collectively support the proposals/projects of the sponsors/developers by investing in the project.

3. **The Platform (the Entity).** The project/proposal is supported by an organization that brings together the project and the people through an online platform.

The Project

Properties such as shopping centers, office or industrial business parks, or mixed-use sites that can benefit from *financial-only* methods to add value are prime candidates for crowdfunding. "Financial only" methods to add value have nothing to do with renovations or upgrading infrastructure. Financial-only methods focus on restructuring the terms and financing to boost the financial performance of the property. Crowdfunding smaller-scale projects like single-family or smaller multi-unit residential properties has yet to fully emerge. Given the demand for capital for small site projects, it's likely to only be a matter of time before some enterprising companies will meet that demand.

The People

The "crowd" is now made up of both accredited and nonaccredited investors. (Prior to the Title IV rulings of the JOBS Act, only accredited investors could invest.) Accredited investors are individuals who earn more than $200,000 per year or have a net worth of over $1 million or entities with over $5 million in assets. The new rules broaden the definition of "qualified investors" to include nonaccredited investors, but caps are placed on how much they can invest. Nonaccredited investors can invest a maximum 10 percent of their income/net worth per year. The intent is to protect less experienced investors and ensure they don't "sell the farm" with a single crowdfunded investment.

The Platform

For those looking for out-of-the-box financing, the crowdfunded, layered funding model can be a viable option. To make it happen, you need the platform. Any quick web search will turn up dozens of sites that can facilitate funding from the crowd using their platform. But not all crowdfunding sites are created equal. Some offer investments only to accredited investors. Some support only specific types of properties and projects in specific geographic areas. Some offer only debt or equity funding, not both. Due diligence is in order before choosing.

When Does It Make Sense to Crowdfund a Deal?

With banking being what it is today, obtaining funding for ambitious projects can be a laborious drain on time and resources. Crowdfunding is a viable alternative for properties that need increased leverage at a lower cost than banks or traditional equity partners offer, and because the process of crowdfunding deals is streamlined, it can often be done in a fraction of the time of the traditional bank/partners route.

A crowdfunding platform also helps you source intelligent funding: Investors are vetted and verified, making for a reliable, one-stop shop for attracting multiple sources of capital. The platform manages all investor relationships for you and pools all accredited investors into a single entity that is a limited liability company (LLC).

The investor management and communications, reporting, updates, and education is left to the crowdfunding platform's team, including attorneys, accounting and financial professionals, and support staff.

What About Debt vs. Equity?

Real estate crowdfunding has two subgroups: debt and equity.

Debt Investment

The participating investor acts as a lender, not an owner of the property. The investor is entitled to monthly interest and return of any unpaid principal at maturity. But debt investors do not receive the benefit of property appreciation. The investment is secured by the property, and if the borrower fails to perform, the investors have recourse and can recover their investment through foreclosure.

Equity Investment

In this case, the investor is an indirect owner of the property. The investor is not secured by the real property and has little recourse if the property doesn't perform. The added risk means the investor is entitled to a greater return, which is generally achieved through property appreciation and then realized when the property is sold.

When considering crowdfunding your deal, the structuring of debt and equity is critical and depends on a wide range of factors, including project type, timing, and market conditions.

The Cost to Raise Capital Through a Crowdfunding Platform

Beyond the returns paid to the crowd, this funding model has expenses related to the facilitation of the funding. Costs will vary depending on the platform, but in general expect fees for establishing and managing the fund that invests in your project.

There will be legal, accounting, compliance, and administrative costs. The platform will put together a marketing package with profiles of the developer and the investment to showcase investment experience, credentials, credibility, past projects, successful turnarounds, rebranding, or leasing results, all in an effort to generate a strong response by investors for your project.

Crowdfunding is still in its infancy but stands to become a standard for funding, and as such, it promises to disrupt the entrepreneurial capital market in a more fundamental way, bringing change to the previously elite world of investment fundraising and investing that used to be the exclusive domain of only the wealthy.

TAKEAWAYS

- *What is the difference between a* debt *investment and an* equity *investment?*

8

THE NEW KID ON THE BLOCK

Crowdfunding

Is Crowdfunding a Good Option for You?

Crowdfunding, generally speaking, is a way of spreading the risk—and the rewards—of an investment over a larger pool of people. Real estate is now an open market for crowdfunding.

Through an online platform, money is raised for a specific property project and individual investor contributions are pooled as the "crowd" for a common collective project as proposed by the property developer.

All this came about in 2012, when the JOBS Act opened the door for accredited investors to invest in crowdfunded investments. And in 2015, new rules opened up investment opportunities to an even wider pool of small investors.

So now, the "crowd" includes accredited investors—those individuals who earn more than $200,000 per year or have a net worth of over $1 million or entities with over $5 million in assets—as well as "qualified investors" who are nonaccredited investors, although caps are placed on how much they can invest. Nonaccredited investors can invest a maximum 10 percent of their income/net worth per year—a governor rule with the intent of protecting the less experi-enced investor's capital.

Pooling your money with other investors spreads the risk while also allowing smaller investors to participate in capital funding once reserved only for the super wealthy.

Why Do It?

- Pooling your money with other investors obviously spreads the risk while also allowing smaller investors to participate in capital funding once reserved only for the super wealthy and well connected.
- Through crowdfunding, investors can make smaller incre-mental investments on a variety of properties rather than going "all in" on just one large property.
- Crowdfunding frees up time and resources. There's no need to get involved in the day-to-day administration or ongoing costs of owning a property.
- Crowdfunded properties offer flexibility that real estate investment trusts (REITs) and similar investment vehicles don't. You can choose the best opportunities to suit your investment objectives and risk profile.
- Through crowdfunding, smaller investors can participate in projects that are not usually accessible to the general public, such as commercial property developments.
- Locating crowdfunded investment opportunities is as easy as a web search. And unlike other investments, there are no costs associated with investing in a project beyond the capital investment itself. So you are saving time and money.

How to Participate in a Crowdfunded Property

When choosing an investment, finding it is only half the battle. You have to vet the projects and developers, looking for a solid track record. Before you jump in, there are a few important things you should know.

One is that you won't really own real estate.

Investing in a crowdfunded real estate investment does not actually make you an owner of real estate. Rather, you become a member of a limited liability company that in turn holds title to real property (in the case of equity) or makes a loan secured by real property (in the case of debt). Your ownership in the LLC is considered personal property rather than real property, and your right to share in the income generated at the property is set forth in a governing document for the LLC called an *operating agreement.*

In addition, when considering crowdfunding your own deal, the structuring of debt and equity is critical and depends on a wide range of factors including project type, timing, and market conditions.

When Are Returns Received?

Crowdfunding real estate sites sell investments in small chunks, which are much more accessible to an average investor than an entire building or development. An investor may contribute $5,000, for example, to purchase an empty building. The funds then go into renovating and leasing out the building, at which time the investor will receive an agreed-on percentage of rents and revenue.

How Do Investors Earn Returns?

When an investor funds a *debt investment opportunity* (usually in the first position and secured by a commercial real estate asset or property), the fund invested in receives monthly interest payments. A share of these payments is deposited directly into a bank account of the investor's choice in accordance with the terms of the operating agreement for the fund.

If funding is made in an *equity investment opportunity* (such as a commercial property or portfolio of properties), the fund invested in will receive periodic payments of cash flow from rents and/or a share of the proceeds when/if a property or portfolio is sold. Similar to debt instruments, a share of those payments will be deposited directly into the investor's selected bank account in accordance with the terms of the operating agreement for the fund. Both investment sponsors and investors must carefully review the operating agreement for the specific investment opportunity that is being considered and offered to investors for further information.

Due Diligence

As with any investment strategy, it is essential that investors do their homework before investing their hard-earned cash. This means looking into the experience and track record of the real estate developers who are soliciting crowdfunded money.

Good developers who have a proven track record of earning substantial returns for their investors would likely not have a difficult time securing funding from a more traditional source, like a bank or a seasoned investment firm. It is worth considering why a developer is going the crowdfunded route. Have they had trouble securing funding because of unsuccessful past projects? If so, what evidence is there that things will be different this time? Have they simply tapped out existing funding sources and need more capital for a viable project? Investors should seek to obtain as much information about a developer's history, including past projects, specific details of the proposed development, and even tax returns in order to make an informed decision about the investment.

🏠 TAKEAWAYS

- *When does it make sense to crowdfund a deal?*
- *When does the equity investor see returns?*
- *When does the debt investor see returns?*

PARTNERING
TO GET THE FUNDS YOU NEED

When Should Property Investors Consider a Partner to Obtain More Funding?

Partnering has been used in real estate as far back as the Roman Empire and maybe even earlier. History is great, but what are the advantages of partnering up for real estate investors today? When does it make sense? Who might make good partners? What pitfalls and potholes in the road should be avoided?

Real Estate Partnerships 101

Real estate partnerships have been used by the elite for centuries and are still used by wealthy, sophisticated investors nowadays. Yet partnerships are also one of the most powerful investment tools available for brand-new investors as well.

The concept is simple. A partnership just means two or more investors are working together to achieve a common goal. It can be a money partner and an individual with the time to do the work. It can be a whole circle of money partners and one partner with the expertise and time to create profits in real estate.

There are a variety of ways to set up partnerships. They can be crowdfunded campaigns, informal agreements between personal contacts, limited liability partnerships (LLPs), or limited liability companies (LLCs). Everyone can have equal shares, or they can be divided up depending on the value of each party's contribution. Regardless of the parties involved, every partnership should be inked and signed by every stakeholder.

Advantages of Partnering Up

Why consider bringing in a partner? For a range of reasons that include:

- Providing the "skin in the game" an asset-based lender may require
- Reducing your personal risk in investing
- Spreading your resources across more deals
- Getting the extra funds you need to acquire and complete deals
- Allowing others to participate in your success
- Doing more and bigger real estate deals
- Having more people invested in your success
- Bringing in experienced individuals to help
- Obtaining better terms on financing

Potential Cons of Partnering Up

What might some of the cons of bringing in partners be?

- Having to split the profits
- Giving up control
- Having to assume extra reporting and accounting responsibilities

- Worrying about rogue partners
- Navigating the tax implications

Smart Times to Partner Up

- When scouting for new property deals (i.e., partnering in advance of a deal)
- When launching real estate crowdfunding campaigns
- When other types of financing cannot be used
- When you need to reduce the cost of leverage
- When you need to provide confidence for future investors and lenders
- When it helps to speed up and secure other types of financing
- When you get stuck for cash
- When taking on a new type of real estate deal

In some cases real estate investors simply won't be able to raise all the funds needed to make a deal happen, or at least have the comfortable cushion they desire. In other scenarios, obtaining some partner funds can provide more flexibility, speed, and better profit margins. An example is obtaining a low loan-to-value (LTV) asset-based loan for the acquisition costs and using partner money to make improvements.

Who Can Investors Partner With?

There are a wide range of potential partners out there, including:

- Family members
- Friends
- Local individuals with excess funds
- Other real estate investors

- Real estate investment groups
- Angel investors
- Venture capital firms
- The public crowd of peer and accredited investors
- Local government and real estate and housing organizations

It's usually best to start looking for partners among those already in your network. When you approach others outside your network for funds, they may want to know how many of your friends and family members have or have not backed you, and why.

Reaching out with partnership opportunities to those outside your inner circle can take various forms—everything from online crowdfunding campaigns, to private conversations over lunch with a potential investor, to live pitch events. Some investors create very detailed and lengthy credibility packages and prospectuses. Others work with a handshake.

What and Who to Avoid When Pitching Potential Partners for Money

What don't you want in a real estate partnership? In real estate partnership scenarios, some of the worst nightmares involve:

- Difficult partners who make it hard to make money
- Overly involved partners who drain time and energy
- Partners who may try to kick you out of the deal or company
- Partners who ruin your relationships with other people in the industry
- Partners who may fail to perform, and even steal from your operation

While there may certainly be exceptions when it pays to bring in a more experienced partner to run things, investors can usually avoid these situations by retaining firm control and legal boundaries.

How to Make It Work

Choose Your Partners Wisely

You may not always be able to spot a scoundrel in advance, but some people are obviously going to be a pain to deal with on a daily basis. Others may give signals that their greed may encroach into your pockets. Trust your gut, and avoid all but those people you really feel synergy with. It's not "just business"; this is personal, and relationships are more valuable than money. So recognize when it is better not to jeopardize your relationships with partnerships and joint ventures.

Protect Yourself with Legal Agreements

The top-ten biggest mistakes when dealing with partners center on the legal arrangements and written agreements made . . . or not made. It's amazing how much money can change people. One day someone is your best friend in the world, the next you find out they emptied your bank account, took an extra mortgage out on your property, and skipped town. Even in less extreme cases, simple miscommunication or assumptions that haven't been addressed can become financial nightmares. Make sure everyone is protected with very clear agreements in writing. Spell out the risks, each party's responsibilities, and the remedies. It is worth investing a couple hundred dollars in having an attorney draft an agreement for you— one that you may be able to use as a template for future deals and partnerships.

Ultimately partnerships are just as important and powerful as financing in real estate investment. There can be pitfalls for those who don't take the risks seriously and protect themselves with smart legal structures. Yet, with so many advantages, partnerships certainly shouldn't be ignored. They could be what makes all the difference in getting you to where you want to be, and a lot faster.

TAKEAWAYS

- *When and why would you consider a partnership deal?*
- *When considering your situation, what are the pluses of a partnership?*
- *For you personally, what would be the main disadvantages of a partnership? Are they deal breakers?*

USING BANKS TO FUND
REAL ESTATE INVESTMENTS

Are Banks and Traditional Lenders a Viable Option?

In the recent past, you wouldn't meet many real estate investors who use banks and other traditional mortgage lenders to fund their investments. There are a number of reasons for it and most are the result of the recession and fallout from the housing bubble in the early 2000s.

Let's explore this option and how it might or might not work for you with your investments. Time is of the essence when it comes to great deals on real estate, and more often than not, it takes too long to get approved for most traditional bank loans. For the single-family residential investor, even if you get approval in time, it's likely you will not be afforded the cash necessary to pay for a foreclosure or short sale property—sometimes you'll need to plan to bring up to 40 percent to the closing table depending on the property and your plans for it. It's not entirely impossible to finance your real estate investments using banks, but if you do attempt to go that route, it's best to expect a few bumps along the way (and to have a backup plan)!

What It Takes to Fund Investment Property

Qualifying for a mortgage for an investment property requires more than your typical 20 percent down payment and decent credit. While the requirements to qualify for home loans for your primary residence have undoubtedly gotten stricter since the housing bubble burst, they are still nothing in comparison with the tough requirements to qualify as an investor.

To begin with, if you are going to fund your investments through a bank, you'll need to have some substantial capital saved already. Because you are purchasing an investment property, mortgage insurance won't cover it, and so you need something else to secure your loan. Typically this will be a 25 percent or higher down payment.

You will increase your chances of approval if you can show that you are a strong and qualified borrower. If your credit score is 740 or higher, you are more likely to qualify, as you've shown that you can borrow and pay back loan money with few hiccups during the repayment.

If you already have a mortgage on a rental property and you are looking for the means to fund another one, you are likely to need a higher credit score if you don't want an astronomical interest rate and/or a much higher down payment. Banks have gotten very wary of risky loans, and more and more they are looking for borrowers to have reserve funds to ensure they'll be able to keep paying even if a rental property is vacant.

The easiest way to get financing for an investment property, however, is to get owner-occupant financing instead of investment financing. If you are going to succeed in getting this kind of financing, though, you will have to use the property as your primary residence for a period of time (usually a minimum of a year) before you start renting it out or attempt to sell it. This is, for obvious reasons, not ideal for most real estate investors.

Why Traditional Lenders Have Turned Away from Funding Investors

So why is it so hard to qualify for a mortgage on an investment property? Essentially, banks and other traditional mortgage lenders are not deliberately cracking down on investors—they are just subjecting investors to a lot more regulation than before because of the risks and fallout from past lending practices.

In addition to government regulations and lending guidelines, a lot of banks are also enacting their own restrictions and requirements. Why? Simply because they do not want to be burned again. Prior to 2008, banks were handing out mortgages left and right. It was incredibly easy (comparatively) to get a loan on your primary residence or even for an investment property.

After the housing crash in 2008, the U.S. government put a lot more restrictions and regulations in place for banks seeking to lend money for real estate. Many of these regulations have banks' hands tied. This prevents them from loaning money to people with multiple mortgages who do not pass a series of ultra-strict requirements.

Unfortunately, entirely too many people who could not afford their mortgages were approved for loans. Those people then did not uphold their end of the bargain, and the banks foreclosed on thousands of properties. The massive real estate crash and resulting recession occurred, and since then traditional lenders began making it more difficult for anyone (owner-occupant or investor) to qualify for a mortgage. Banks are in the money business, not the house business, and the crash put them squarely in the middle of owning real estate and having to resell it to recoup their funds.

Finally, a real estate investment is typically a riskier loan than an owner-occupant mortgage. Qualified borrowers who are in the market to buy a home where they'll live typically base their budgets on their income and how much they can afford to pay per month on their mortgage. Basically, their loan payments will be part of their monthly expenses, and the ability to make payments won't be based on some future venture.

This is why it is especially difficult for new investors to get loans from banks for their real estate investments. They may not have the net worth or income to pay on the loan if their investment does not pay off. Conversely, though, this is why it's easier and potentially more lucrative for veteran investors with other streams of income to qualify—in limited cases—for traditional funding.

Pros and Cons

If you are interested in funding your investments through banks and/or other traditional mortgage lenders, you should be aware of a few pros and cons. Considering and weighing each of them will help you get a full understanding of this type of lending and how it may or may not be right for your investments.

Pro: Interest Rates Are Lower

Typically, you'll find the lowest interest rates of all types of investment loans from banks and mortgage lenders. Because they are so strict about who can get a loan, they can set their interest rates much lower than hard money lenders or even private money lenders. And, when compared with splitting your profits 50/50 with a partner, those rates look even better—provided you can get them.

Con: Getting Approval Is Difficult

As I've already emphasized, as an investor it can be incredibly difficult to qualify for a mortgage loan from a bank. Getting approval almost always requires you to have at least a 25 percent down payment on the property, and you'll need to prove that you can make your mortgage payments on time and in full, whether or not you have tenants paying rent on the property. Rental property income isn't based on actual cash flow—it's based on a formula. So, in many cases, investors who were certain they could qualify can't because of how banks calculate investment and rental income. Another qualifier that makes it difficult to get approval is the debt-to-income ratio (DTI). The real estate investor with outstanding debts must be able to meet strict income ratios to offset the lender's risk.

Con: Approval Takes Time

Even when you do qualify for a loan, getting that loan approved and closed takes more time than you can typically afford. When you find a lead on a great investment opportunity and get it under contract, you usually need to fund it as quickly as possible so that you do not lose it. Banks and mortgage lenders are not typically the fastest at getting back to you about approval or getting your funds to you quickly. There are a lot of moving parts and approval processes that most investors don't have the time to deal with.

Con: It's Not Good for Flipping

If you are in the market to fix and flip properties, then this is definitely not the funding opportunity for you. The advantage you have when buying short sales and distressed properties is that you can offer to pay up front and in cash. And, if you are buying foreclosed real estate owned (REO) properties that need a lot of work, a bank mortgage isn't even an option.

Pro: Terms Are Flexible

Again, if you can qualify for a bank loan for your investment, with exemplary credit, a solid track record, and a relationship with your lender, you may also qualify for attractive and/or flexible terms. You might get a variable rate loan that gives you lower payments over a longer period of time, or you might be able to get a low, fixed-rate loan that is easier to pay off, whether or not your investment is currently bringing in cash flow.

Pro and Con: Your Credit Can Work for or Against You

Finally, if you have great credit, you can get better loan terms that will allow you a lot more flexibility and the ability to continue investing your surplus returns in other investments. But just as your good credit can work for you with a bank loan, bad credit will work against you. Without stellar credit, even if you do get approved, you may be looking at terms that just don't work for you and your investment.

As you can see, if you are a seasoned investor with multiple streams of income—especially income that's unrelated to mortgaged properties—borrowing from banks to fund your investments may work, but count on delays, documentation, and challenges. Bank funding is not the ideal solution for most investors, and it can be problematic on a few different levels for newer investors or those who do not have the best credit history.

Alternative Strategy

Despite the challenges most real estate investors face with funding using traditional mortgages, there are potential strategies to make financing work. While it's a current reality that most traditional lenders shy away from distressed, fix and flip properties, it's possible to use a combination of strategies for long-term hold, rental properties.

The idea is relatively simple, but does require careful consideration of the cost of funding. When purchasing distressed properties intended for long-term hold, many investors use hard or private money for the acquisition and renovations. Once the renovation is complete and the property is in service as a rental, the investor can seek out long-term traditional funding. This can work for a number of reasons.

- The value of the property has increased, which impacts appraisals and loan-to-value considerations.
- Debt-to-income ratios can be positively impacted. Once the property is in service and generating income, it can add to the overall positive income picture for the investor seeking to qualify for traditional financing.

Like any financing strategy, it's important to include the closing costs of both funding scenarios into the overall financial analysis of the property.

TAKEAWAYS

- *What are the primary roadblocks to using banks for funding investment real estate?*
- *What will a traditional bank require from the typical investor when considering underwriting a loan?*

HOW TO FIND
ASSET-BASED LENDERS

Asset-based lending has been growing in popularity among both borrowers and lenders. So what are the most efficient and effective ways for real estate investors to find asset-based loans today?

Who Makes Asset-Based Loans?

Asset-based loans are more readily available to individual investors and smaller investment firms than ever before. Today asset-based loans can come from various sources:

- Online portals where pre-vetted lenders compete to fund deals
- Large private equity and hedge funds
- Big national banks
- Regional and community banks
- Family offices
- Hard money lenders

- Crowdfunding portals
- Venture capital firms
- Wealthy private investors
- Average individuals with underperforming capital
- Commercial lenders
- Mortgage lenders
- Specialist lenders

The Traditional Method of Finding Asset-Based Lenders

The traditional, "old school" way of finding lenders for real estate deals typically involved getting all of your paperwork together and then stumping from lender to lender with document after document—with each lender requiring something new and different.

Since these lenders were known to be notoriously slow in processing loan requests, and their requirements often meant lengthy closings, there wasn't much room for shopping around. The time and opportunity just wasn't there, so deals could be hanging by a thread and the lenders could effectively charge what they liked—because the investor needed to get the deal done. Often there were heavy up-front fees without any guarantee of a loan.

At best, real estate investors hoped to have a broker who would streamline the process with additional points added for "rushing" the closing. In other cases, an investor might happen to run into a local lender at an investment group who showed interest. And for those investors with millions of dollars in assets, they might try going through a local private bank, perhaps using their pull to push the loan application to a committee meeting. Put bluntly, this way of finding funding for real estate investing was expensive, inefficient, and highly risky for investor borrowers.

The New Way to Find Asset-Based Loans

Technology has revolutionized just about every aspect of our daily lives. And real estate is no exception. When it comes to locating properties, it's become increasingly clear that most property shoppers use web-based services to locate and close real estate transactions.

The trends by homeowners to use online resources for buying and financing properties extend to investor buyers as well. Technology has risen to meet the demands of today's investor.

In a matter of minutes, real estate investors can complete an online application from their computer or even from a smartphone and the application is sent to multiple lenders to compete to fund the property. Quicker than you can grab a cup of coffee, an investor can submit a loan request to a variety of asset-based lenders who are eager to fund that deal.

This dramatically speeds up the process so investors can get answers on the move, and it enables them to compare and shop great loan offers. This reduces risk in making purchase offers, increases investors' own competitiveness, helps them to be more efficient in operating, and can substantially increase overall net returns.

Lenders value the opportunity to originate loans through new online channels because of the ease and efficiency it affords them. Finding and building relationships with new investor/borrowers used to be an expensive and time-consuming endeavor. But the technology solutions are a win-win for lenders and borrowers alike. Technology creates savings and more profitability from efficient originations. Those savings can be passed on to borrowers, so they can get better terms and rates than ever before.

TAKEAWAYS

- *What are the primary advantages of using "the new way" to find asset-based lenders for your real estate investments?*

12

INSIDE THE MIND OF
ASSET-BASED LENDERS

What Do You Need to Know to Get Your Deal Funded?

The business of hard money, asset-based lending is all about the numbers—but that's not the whole story. When you are considering using asset-based funding, you need to understand the mindset of lenders: What are they looking for in the property, the project, and the project's principal . . . you, the investor?

Lenders of all types use the rule of "the six C's" when considering funding a property. Their goal is to minimize risk while still making money. Lenders are not just looking for higher yields, they're looking for safe, secure investments that return capital and a solid return on investment (ROI). They want to know how and when they'll be paid back and they like to build repeat business with investors, so relationship building is key.

Lenders often use a "decision matrix" to help guide them in deciding whether to underwrite a loan. Most use the six C's to make an initial determination if the property, the project, and the principals can stand up to the rigors of the underwriting process.

The Six C's

1. **Collateral.** Lenders are in the money business, not the real estate business. They will carefully consider all aspects of the property—its physical condition, its marketability, and its profit potential, among others—all to determine what kind of equity cushion the property offers in its loan-to-value (LTV).

2. **Capacity.** Lenders will look for assurance that the borrower has the capacity to carry out the terms of the loan. They will look at experience, outcomes, partnerships, resources, and existing obligations of the borrower.

3. **Character.** Many lenders also look into the character of the potential borrower. They may do background checks looking for liens and judgments, criminal background, and other derogatory public records.

4. **Conditions.** To minimize risk, many lenders look carefully into the conditions surrounding the property: How is the market in the target investment area? What is the availability of resources and other property inventory? Is there demand for the property at resale or rental?

5. **Capital.** The whole notion of "no money down" in real estate investing is misleading. No-money-down transactions are rare—and nearly nonexistent with most lenders. While it is possible to have none of your own money down, lenders still require that the borrower have skin in the game in the form of a down payment.

6. **Credit.** With asset-based lending, credit isn't most important but it still plays a role. Good credit can make the difference between a yes and a no; it's really a matter of how good (or bad) the borrower's other five C's look to the lender.

There's flexibility, so don't be overly concerned if you are a new investor. Maybe you don't have the capacity of a more experienced investor, but you've got great collateral, character, capital, credit, and conditions. You're still in the running; you just may need to bring a little more equity or capital to the table.

What Scares Lenders Away?

Money is attracted to opportunity, not people. Lenders are looking for the opportunity to make money loaning you money. Investors just getting started don't have the pedigree, but that alone won't scare off lenders. What you have to do is "show them the money." Despite a lender's eagerness to profit, there are lots of other things related to the six C's that can scare off a lender.

The Collateral

In the lender's mind, the thought is, "Would I want to own this real estate if there's a default?" Location and condition can be a factor. The value plays a major role. The appraisal comes in and it's not good. Was the after-repair value (ARV) too low? Were the costs of repairs too high? You have to be realistic about your numbers.

Your Capacity

Borrowers who can't demonstrate a clear ability to repay the loan—either through their own resources or those of others—will be a "no way" flag for a lender.

Your Character

Deals gone bad, unpaid debts, criminal activity—these problems and more can derail funding. Some lenders sell the notes they write, so they are looking for solid performance and good business practices.

The Conditions

Market conditions and geographics can cause a lender to turn away. Not all lenders loan in all locations and asset classes.

Capital

The notion of "no money down" is a misnomer. Using a partner, it's possible to use none of *your own* money. Lenders will require skin in the game, however, so expect to bring money to closing—either your own or someone else's—to get your deal closed.

Your Credit

A compromised (or nonexistent) credit score isn't reason for denial alone, but it weighs into the pros and cons of the rest of the loan application.

What If You Can't Repay?

Before issuing funds, asset-based lenders will vet the property and the numbers thoroughly. You have to always remember that they are in the loan business, not in the real estate business, and they do not want to foreclose and become property owners. But sometimes deals go bad. Lenders will respond more positively to possible workout solutions with borrowers who keep the lines of communication open, which is preferred to a costly foreclosure. Some lenders can offer loan modifications, extensions, and other possible solutions. This topic is covered in more detail in Chapter 39.

What's Your Next Step?

Understand that companies that lend money on residential investment properties need you just as much as you need them. *Billions* of dollars have been raised and are available to help you grow your real estate investing empire. The key is understanding lenders' criteria and developing relationships of mutual benefit.

TAKEAWAYS

- *List the six things that will scare away an asset-based lender.*

ASSET-BASED LENDERS

A Peek at Their Cards

What More Do You Need to Know About How They Operate?

Asset-based lenders (also known as hard and private money real estate lenders) are in the game of lending money for one reason only: to profit. Their goal is to work on behalf of the individuals and institutions that entrust them with their capital that is, in turn, loaned to you, the real estate investor. The lender is charged with deploying that capital and putting it to use to make a profit for those who provide the money to loan. Lenders are always working in the best interest of their investors/capital partners, because without them, they have no money to loan.

How Asset-Based Lenders Make Money and How It Works to Fund Your Deal

Each lender you approach for funding works differently. Though all lenders have regulations they must follow, they set their own rates, terms, and underwriting guidelines within the parameters of the law. It's incumbent on you to find the best match between the lender and your property and project.

> Despite the fact that lenders are really on the side of their capital partners, it's important to remember that the lender needs you, too. Without real estate investors, a lender's business model is one-sided. Lenders may have capital, but without you and your willingness to work with the terms, guidelines, and conditions they require, it's no more effective than the cash stashed under Granny's mattress. It earns them nothing.

Key Areas Where Asset-Based Lenders and Their Capital Partners Make Money

It's important to remember there are two key players at the table that stand to profit from the proceeds of your loan. First, there's the capital investor who has provided the funds to loan; this investor's profit (in general) comes from the interest earned during the loan period. Capital investors may also profit from origination points. These are percentages charged to you up front for the opportunity to get your property funded.

Of course, these are just generalities; each lender and each capital investor sets terms that meet their particular objectives, and there may be other profit centers not mentioned here. Typically, you as the real estate investor will never have contact with the capital partner and, in fact, will have no knowledge of who is actually backing your loan with cash.

Second, there's the entity that you work with to fund your deal. This lender makes money a number of ways. One way is origination points (as already mentioned); the lender may also profit from servicing fees. Servicing fees are fees charged to you that pay for the work to service your loan: everything from processing payments to closing the loan when it is repaid in full.

Lenders also make money if and when they sell your note to another entity. There are also a number of other fees a lender may charge, so be sure to review any offer to fund your property and inquire about every fee. In general, though certainly not in every case, the lender does not profit from interest rates; the interest is usually paid to the capital partners as compensation for loaning their cash. But there are always exceptions.

It's also important to note that the lender is the middle man and, as such, bears a huge responsibility for loaning the capital effectively so that earnings are maximized. Chapter 12, "Inside the Mind of Asset-Based Lenders," discussed what a lender looks for from you as the borrower. Asset-based lenders can be an invaluable piece of the puzzle for the real estate investor.

Getting to know the ins and outs of asset-based loans and lenders is critical. It pays to talk to as many lenders as possible. Get referrals from other investors and use online sources to get multiple lenders competing to fund your deal. Know that fees can be negotiated, and don't get so caught up in the need to fund a property that you don't negotiate better terms. If you know how to get great deals on properties, you should also know how to get deals on your funding.

TAKEAWAYS

- *What are the most important things for real estate investors to understand about asset-based lenders?*

14

DEALING WITH DOWN PAYMENTS

Most traditional real estate loans have pretty strict qualifying requirements these days: The borrower must have good credit history, reasonable income that's verifiable, a low debt-to-income ratio, and a big down payment.

However, we're not talking about traditional real estate loans; we're talking about asset-based loans—hard and private money loans specifically for real estate investment that are based on the value of the asset (the property). So credit history isn't a deal breaker, personal income isn't a deal breaker, debt-to-income won't kill the deal, and down payments aren't quite as important—although more often than not, there is still a down payment requirement.

One way hard and private money lenders protect themselves is with lower loan-to-value (LTV) ratios. So, for example, a lender whose requirement is 65 percent LTV would loan you $65,000 on a property whose value is determined to be $100,000 after repairs. But let's say you found property that you can purchase for $70,000 that needs minimal repairs to resell at $100,000. Your lender would require that you bring $5,000 to the table so that the loan is only $65,000—or 65 percent LTV.

 The whole notion of "no money down" is a stretch. Sure, it may not be *your* money, but asset-based lenders want borrowers to have skin in the game. This can be in the form of equity in the property, but expect that the lender will want some sort of down payment as well.

When you're faced with having to make down payments to close your deals, what's the best way to access the cash needed to get you in the game? Investors can get pretty creative when it comes to financing, and the same is true of securing down payments. A word of caution here: No matter where you are sourcing your funds, you *must* understand the numbers. In the case of fix and flips, does the deal support the cost of financing it, repairing it, and selling it? Too many investors, especially new investors, forget to include the cost of money in their calculations. For long-term holds, does the net operating income support the cost of the money after you've deducted all of the expenses of owning and renting out the property?

Five Ways to Secure a Down Payment for Real Estate Investment

Once you know that the numbers work, you can tap into various sources to get your down payment to close the deal.

Your Own Cash or Resources

Naturally, if you have cash set aside, you can use that. It's the cheapest money you can access—and the easiest. When you consider the cost of borrowed money—for simplicity, let's say it is 7 percent interest—then using the money you have sitting in a bank earning .02 percent is a pretty good deal. Better to lose .02 percent than pay 7 percent.

But if you don't have cash set aside, you can:

1. **Borrow from your IRA.** Many individual retirement accounts have no-penalty short-term loans. Do your homework and understand all the terms and conditions of repayment.

2. **Use your own credit.** Many investors will tap into their credit cards or other lines of credit. Again, do your homework, *run the numbers* (does the cost of this money fit into the deal?), and know the terms and conditions of repayment and build it into your deal. Expect the debt incurred to impact underwriting—lenders will look at all of your obligations.

3. **Use existing equity.** Similarly, many investors use their own home's equity to jumpstart their deals. An open-ended home equity line of credit (HELOC) can give you readily accessible cash for purchases, repairs, and down payments. But again, know your numbers and make sure you can stick to the repayment terms.

4. **Borrow against assets.** If you own cars, boats, motorcycles, or any other asset of considerable value, you can use it as collateral for getting the cash for down payments. The sources of that cash are varied—it could be a friend, family member, or even a bank or credit union.

5. **Use OPM (other people's money).** When you don't have personal resources to bring money to the closing table, you have the option to use other people's money.

- Borrow from someone else's IRA. Just like you can borrow from your own IRA, you can borrow from another person's IRA. This strategy usually requires that the individual has a self-directed IRA in place (especially if you need a quick closing). But the other person may also be able to borrow short-term from a traditional IRA. Just make sure everyone in the deal understands all the terms and conditions. Go into the deal with eyes wide open and you may be able to do repeat deals with other people's money.
- Bring in a partner. Partnerships, per se, can be tricky beasts and when not well executed, they can cost you a

lot of money. Keep it simple—because really, all you need is down payment money, so don't give away the farm. Offer your partner a fair and reasonable interest rate and repayment terms. Secure your partner's loan with collateral—either a second mortgage on the subject property (your asset-based lender will have the first mortgage) or offer other collateral as security for the loan. Looking for a partner? Search real estate investors in your area through your local Real Estate Investors Association (REIA) and social media sites.

The bottom line is this: If you have a great deal on a property, remember "money finds opportunity." Many investment property financing options are out there, and rather than going into any deal with a beggar's mindset, approach it from an opportunity mindset. Good deals on real estate create lots of opportunity—for you as the fix and flipper or landlord, and for potential lenders who can make interest income from the opportunities you present when you need a little bit of down payment cash to make a deal happen.

TAKEAWAYS

- *When considering your own sources of down payments, which of those mentioned in this chapter could work for you?*
- *Which OPM strategies hold possibilities, and what do you need to do to tap into them?*

THE DIRTY TRUTH ABOUT
SOME REAL ESTATE LENDERS

Are You Ready for the Truth?

The sad truth is that not all real estate lenders are trustworthy. It's a truth that impacts all businesses, not just the lending business. So how can real estate investors get the financial leverage they need and avoid becoming victims of unscrupulous lenders?

The Unstoppable Money Machine

Clearly, not all lenders, banks, and finance professionals are bad. In the wake of the financial crises in the early part of the 2000s, many people developed a negative opinion of banks and lenders, especially those who finance real estate. But now more lenders have entered the industry with the express purpose of changing things for the better by tapping into a market of borrowers who were left underserved following the crash. Still, overall the lending industry deliberately, blatantly, repeatedly (and even systematically) disregarded the rules, to the pain and loss of the public.

It was the fallout of the financial crisis that led to the biggest banks and mortgage lenders being blamed for appraisal fraud, mortgage fraud, and discriminatory and predatory lending practices. Add to that the massive robo-signing scandal in which at least hundreds of thousands of homes were illegally put into foreclosure and you've got a wary borrowing public.

Eight Common Lender Scams

Banking and lending giants can be considered just too big to control. They are massive money-making machines that derive much of their compounding profits from real estate and mortgage lending. When borrowing money for real estate, it's a matter of staying safe by knowing some of the common tricks and scams and looking for better lending partners.

1. **Up-front Money Scams.** One of the most common scams that can particularly impact real estate investors are lenders that demand up-front fees and then fail to deliver a loan. Or at least a loan that works. This money may be called virtually anything: from application fees to broker fees to inspection fees. There are third-party hard costs to almost all loans. When possible, investors should only pay these fees directly to the third-party vendors providing the service. Some "lenders" may otherwise make a ton of money without giving out any loans at all.

2. **Taking Your Deals.** While hard to prove, some mortgage brokers and investors believe that lenders may actually be dragging out their requests and denying them in order to scoop the deals for themselves. Clearly, reputable lenders whose focus is on loaning money, not owning real estate, are the safer bet.

3. **Bait and Switch.** Perhaps the most common scam of all is bait and switch. In fairness, this sometimes occurs simply due to poorly trained and inexperienced loan officers. In other cases

it is a systematic process of giving lowball quotes to get loan applications in the door and then expecting to hold borrowers captive through the closing, no matter what the terms end up being. After all, what are you going to do at closing, when your contract is expiring and your only choice is to take a higher interest rate or walk away from your deposit money and possibly get sued?

4. **Freezing Credit Lines.** Reverse mortgage advisers revealed that one of the largest banks in the United States became subject to a class-action lawsuit after freezing borrower lines of credit after the credit was granted in order to try to reduce their figures. The last thing you want after you've jumped through the hoops to get money is to have the well cut off.

5. **Forced-Placed Insurance.** Forced-placed insurance scams perpetrated by real estate lenders and servicers have been some of the ugliest and most devastating for borrowers. After closing (which requires proof of insurance), borrowers receive notices that the lender lost the record and has now placed insurance of their choosing on the property, often to the tune of thousands of dollars. Future payments by borrowers are then first credited to the scam insurance, while mortgage payments go "unpaid" until the borrower pays the ransom money or loses the property to foreclosure.

6. **Mortgage Relief Scams.** Mortgage relief scams are often perpetrated by lenders and loan servicers under the guise of loan modification and short-sale help. Struggling borrowers are encouraged to apply for this assistance, only to have their requests drawn out until the lender forecloses at a moment that is most profitable for the lender.

7. **Illegal Foreclosures.** The robo-signing scandal has been one of the largest mortgage scams of all time. This scam involves lenders fraudulently signing documents to illegally foreclose on properties they made loans on, in order to seize and resell the underlying real estate.

8. **Gurus with Paper.** The tightening of capital in the past led real estate investors to look for funding in the most unusual of places. One strategy that was cooked up by so-called real estate gurus promises funding for deals when, in reality, the guru collects a handsome sum from the investor and provides nothing more than a useless proof-of-funds letter that only allows the investor to make an offer. After that, the investor is roped into a partnership deal that can turn a good project into a bad one.

Chapter 16 covers the safeguards you can take to protect yourself from hard money scams.

Overpromise and Underdeliver

Good businesses and professionals underpromise and overdeliver. They don't claim to do it. They just do it, and the results for everyone involved are better. Unfortunately, some real estate investors may encounter quite the opposite tactics out there at roadshows and events run by real estate investment gurus. Some of them promise access to money to fund deals. Not all deliver, or they have lenders with criteria so tight that it is hard to obtain. The majority of these gurus and events often simply refer attendees and students to third-party asset-based lenders that people can find locally or online by themselves.

There are also many lead generation websites out there that encourage users to enter their information to get a loan quote but are not operated by lenders and do not directly connect investors with lending sources. Rather, these pages are often just run by marketing companies to collect lead information that is bundled and resold to a variety of firms. Often these can be spotted as one-page landing pages with no substantial company information and no real contact information.

Tips for Finding Lenders You Can Trust

- Look up reviews.
- Ask for referrals.
- Seek loan officers looking for long-term business relationships.
- Choose loan officers who actually take their time to understand your financing needs and goals and scenario, rather than throwing out blind quotes.

Protect yourself well in the process by selecting reputable lenders (note that bigger isn't always better). Allow plenty of time to close, carefully review the Closing Disclosure, build relationships for repeat business, and refuse to be a victim of bad lenders that go on and hurt others and the real estate market.

TAKEAWAYS

- *How can you locate reputable lenders?*

16

HARD MONEY LENDER SCAMS
AND HOW TO AVOID THEM

We've said it before and it's worth repeating . . . money follows opportunity. We've seen it happening in real estate investing, especially in the single-family residential market where big money (Wall Street) has entered the arena. We are also seeing in it the hard money lending game as well.

A massive amount of new capital is available for real estate investors from traditional and nontraditional sources. But not all lenders are created equal—and with this renewed interest in loaning money to real estate investors comes the potential for hard money lender scams.

Here's what you need to look out for so that your deal gets funded and you don't waste time or, even worse, get ripped off by an opportunist who is not a verified and reputable real estate lender. Here are the most common problems that investors encounter when seeking funding and how to avoid them.

Fees

All lenders charge fees—it's a cost of doing business. But does the lender charge nonrefundable up-front application fees? Are lenders charging due diligence fees? Travel fees? "Boots on the ground" fees? And are all of these fees charged whether or not the loan closes? If so, this is a clear sign that the company is making money on fees, *not* on closed loans. Do your homework before paying a lender up-front fees.

Safeguards

► Ask lenders what percentage of their revenue comes from fees versus closed loans.

► Require the lender to sign an agreement that fees paid up front are fully refundable in the event the loan doesn't close.

► Pay for appraisals, surveys, and other due diligence outside closing to avoid "fee padding" and other fee scams.

Johnny Come Lately

Be on the lookout for the posers. There are so-called private money brokers trying to capitalize on today's opportunities. Investors can't afford to lose both time and money when trying to secure funding, so it's worth the effort to vet and verify your lender's credentials. If you encounter a private hard money lender, ask for credentials. A credible lender will be a Certified Private Money Broker.

Safeguards

► Ask how many loans they've closed. They should be able to demonstrate a track record of success.

► Get at least three names and phone numbers of recent past clients. Call these customers and ask about their experience with the broker.

As in just about any industry, there are good and bad players. It's the same with hard money lenders and private money brokers. It is always wise to approach lenders with a "borrower beware" mindset. Some good advice from our fortieth president, Ronald Reagan: "Trust but verify."

TAKEAWAYS

- *What are the safeguards you can use to avoid scams?*

17

HOW TO SUCCESSFULLY
GET FUNDED AS A NEW INVESTOR

f you are without experience, are there extra hoops you'll have to jump through? Extra pitfalls to watch out for? How can the funding process be made easier?

Getting financing for real estate investment properties can be a bit more challenging for new investors. Lenders are typically much more comfortable with experienced investors who have a track record of successful real estate investing activities. Getting a foot in the door can be a challenge, and there can also be underwriting challenges for new investors who lack knowledge and experience. And there may be predators out there looking to prey on new real estate investors who don't recognize the red flags in a bad deal. The good news for the new investor is that there are also solutions for adequately funding real estate investment properties.

Specific Challenges Facing Newer
Real Estate Investors

- Limited number of loans available until track record is proven
- Payment shock

- Inability to use history of income from real estate to qualify
- Down payments
- Reserve requirements
- Being unwittingly lured into committing real estate and mortgage fraud

In a nutshell, the lack of a track record means that individual lenders will be much more cautious about how much money they will loan to begin "experimenting." And although asset-based loans are primarily underwritten based on the property, lenders are extra cautious with new investors who've yet to turn a property into profits. It's mostly common sense, but these can be barriers that many new investors don't expect; most mistakenly think that their great deal is all that's needed to get funded.

The best defense for the new investor is to ask a lot of questions, know your mortgage terminology, consult with others who are more experienced, and don't be afraid to do some comparison shopping.

What to Look for in a Real Estate Lender

- An investor-friendly lender who wants to do your type of deals
- A lender and loan officer serious about building a relationship
- A loan officer who asks the right questions
- A lender who does not charge upfront fees
- A lender who is responsive
- A lender who's honest about lending guidelines and the potential to offer a loan

You've got to find the right lender match, beginning with someone who specializes in funding your type of deals, or the process will be painfully slow at best. And we all know that good deals require quick action. More than one deal has been lost due to financing hiccups.

Your loan officer should care about building a relationship. Look for those serious about asking the right questions and who provide references from past and current clients. Ask for references from other industry professionals like title companies and realtors.

Great loan officers won't just ask the questions needed to fill in the blanks on a mortgage application. They should ask what you want to achieve and what your longer-term plans are. That way, they can truly provide loan options that best empower those plans.

How to Improve Your Funding Success as a New Investor

Improve your attractiveness as a borrower by:

- Doing your homework. Don't wait until you have a deal in hand that has to close quickly. Start researching and building lender relationships before you need them.
- Submitting strong loan applications. Applications must be complete and honest. Make the lender's job easier.
- Bringing in a partner with experience, stronger financials, better credit, and cash.
- Being pleasant to deal with and always prepared.
- Being patient in scaling your investments. Rome wasn't built in a day, and neither is a solid real estate investment track record.

Follow this advice and you can look forward to easier borrowing, streamlined processes, and even preferred terms. It is possible to go from zero to hero and have lenders fight for your business.

Chapter 9 on partnering and Chapter 14 on dealing with down payments cover more on this topic.

🏠 TAKEAWAYS

- *What steps can a new investor take to secure first-time funding?*

18

HOW TO LAND THE BEST LOANS FOR YOUR DEALS

Finding the Best Financing for Investment Property

There is a lot of money out there, and there are a lot of people and institutions who want to put that money to work generating more money. Success in real estate investment and maximizing the profit potential of each deal means obtaining the optimal loan for your property and project. So how do investors make sure they find the best loan for real estate investment?

What's So Important About Finding the Right Loan?

Finding the right money for real estate investment makes all the difference in successfully executing your plan for any specific property and in determining how much your net profit will be.

Not every loan or line of credit you land is going to be at the very lowest market rates or come with your personal dream terms. But finding the right money for real estate investment makes all the difference in successfully executing your plan for the property and in determining how much your net profit will be. It's also critical to know that a loan exists for your strategy even before making an offer. Knowing the available loan programs helps you swiftly navigate the entire process, from deal search through negotiations, offer, and closing. Having baseline knowledge of your funding sources can give you a serious speed, efficiency, and profit edge over competitors for quality deals in your market.

How to Match Loans and Lenders to Your Needs

Each real estate investment loan or line of credit should take you closer to your individual deal goals and your big-picture vision. Factors to keep in mind when loan shopping include:

- Protecting your credit score for further deals
- Protecting credit bandwidth for future deals
- Sustainability: lenders who help build a lasting foundation for your business
- Maintaining enough liquidity, equity, and time to exit
- Obtaining enough money and credit to get the deal finished
- Securing deep-enough margins to maintain profitability over the long term
- Speed and ease of funding
- Reliability of closing on time
- Trustworthiness of the lender
- Exit costs
- Having the ability to use the entity you want to finance under
- Ensuring the right lender and loan match for the property type, location, and strategy

Financing a Real Estate Investment Using Different Real Estate Strategies

Real Estate Wholesaling

Real estate wholesalers typically seek out equity-based loans and transactional "quick turn" lenders that can provide funding for the very short term. The wholesaler's goal (when not doing a simple contract assignment) is to close on the acquisition and immediately resell the property. Transactional lenders understand the dynamics of wholesaling and the disrepair that wholesale properties are often in. In addition, savvy wholesalers who are assigning contracts have connections with lenders that they can refer for their wholesale buyers.

Buy and Hold Real Estate Investing

There are two approaches to financing buy and hold income properties. One is purchasing existing rentals, and the other is rehabbing a distressed property and then leasing it out. Investment properties in need of substantial work or that require additional funds to make repairs may require a rehab loan followed by a longer-term loan. On the other hand, properties ready for long-term, permanent financing may benefit from more conventional financing or blanket mortgages from the initial acquisition.

Fix and Flip Deals

Fix and flip deals will often require rehab loans that include funding for acquisition, holding, and improvements. Most traditional lenders aren't interested in funding these types of short-term loans, so investors are wise to seek out asset-based lenders and hard money lenders who offer equity-based loans.

New Construction Financing

There are two main types of loans for new construction properties. Investor financing for real estate includes "end loans" for those acquiring completed units complete with a Certificate of Occupancy from the developer. Construction loans are for financing the actual building of units. There are also "one-time close" construction-to-permanent loans, which automatically roll over into fixed-rate financing once building is complete and the collateral exists to secure the loan.

Commercial Real Estate Loans

Commercial mortgage loans have traditionally been used for financing five-plus-unit multifamily properties, industrial property, office buildings, and retail real estate. However, since 2008, more commercial lenders are loaning on residential homes for investment purposes. These lenders and loans often suit those financing property for "business" purposes and want to finance properties under the names of limited liability companies (LLCs), corporations, and trusts. It's important for real estate investors to know that traditional lenders will not lend on properties held in an LLC or other entity.

Land Loans for Development

Many banks and other lenders make land loans. They can range from loans for individual lots to large blanket loans for raw land that may be subdivided. Loan-to-value ratios (LTVs) are typically significantly lower than for improved properties. Some lenders have provisions requiring borrowers to begin building within a certain time frame, refinance, or pay off their loans.

Business Loans

Real estate investors can also use general business loans to fund deals. The application and approval process is very different from an asset-based loan. The loan is not based on collateral but instead is based on experience and potential earnings as well as other factors. The lender will want you and your partner(s) to demonstrate good character, have experience and good personal and/or business credit history, along with the capacity to repay the loan.

Comparing Loans for Your Real Estate Deals

It is important to get the hang of apples-to-apples comparisons for loan shopping. You can compare oranges too. But you need to understand the difference. The best way to compare real estate loans is with the Lending Estimate provided by lenders. This document shows all the costs, loan features, and true annual percentage rate (APR) or cost of borrowing. Use this to compare different quotes side by side. Don't just look at the bottom-line figures; make sure each feature line item is the same for an apples-to-apples comparison.

Quick Tips for Quickly Homing in on the Best Loan Programs

1. Know that it doesn't always just take one loan or type of funding.
2. Reread and get to know Lending Estimate forms.
3. Watch out for prepayment penalties, adjustable rates, and balloons that lenders fix into your exit strategy.
4. Make sure your lender likes loaning in your area, on your property type.
5. Create spreadsheets or keep track of loan parameters, so you can instantly match potential deals with the right lenders and enjoy a stress-free closing.
6. Know the terms. When buying real estate, it's "location, location, location." When financing real estate, it's all about the terms, terms, terms. Know which terms affect your bottom line and *how*. You may get a great rate, but if the

loan is called due ahead of your exit timeline, it's not the right loan.

The bottom line? Know your lender, know their loans, and more important, know which terms are most important for your property, project, and exit strategy.

 TAKEAWAYS

- *What are the main criteria you will use to match lenders to your investment needs?*

19

IS YOUR BABY UGLY?

The Due Diligence Steps Every Real Estate Investor Should Take

How do you know if you are really onto a good real estate deal and should invest? What due diligence should property investors engage in before presenting the deal to potential lenders?

Everyone Thinks Their Baby Is Beautiful

Beauty is definitely in the eye of the beholder. When it comes to investing in real estate, investors need to look beyond the property and test their optimism with real, fact-based due diligence. Investors need to make sure the opportunity will be profitable and that it's attractive to the lender. Not every deal is a good deal. You've got to see the property for what it is—and what it isn't.

How to Screen for Money Makers

Here are six quick steps for making smart real estate acquisitions:

1. Make sure the deal matches your investment and acquisition criteria.
2. Optimize your processes. These processes are screening and making offers on properties, and arranging funding.
3. Follow smart principles and use formulas and common sense (don't get caught up in the excitement of the deal). Run the numbers using the formulas in Chapter 22, check your assumptions, and run it past a partner or colleague.
4. Verify the numbers before making an offer.
5. Present the deal to the right lender(s).
6. Dig in and complete the due diligence and closing.

Investors simply can't waste their time looking at every available property. No matter what your level of experience, you should have some basic criteria of what you are looking for. This way you spend your time on the most viable opportunities that fit your investment objectives. These criteria include:

- Location and marketability
- Square feet of living area
- Price range
- Potential profit spread or rental income
- Number of bedrooms
- Property type
- Complexity of repairing and remarketing the property

 Investors need to make sure not only that the opportunity will be profitable but also that it is attractive to lenders.

If properties don't match your criteria, your marketing and due diligence should reflect that. Any referral sources should have a good idea of your buying criteria. If you are marketing through your website, your messaging should target the kinds of houses you are looking for, so you attract good quality prospects. Serious volume investors often have acquisition assistants to screen for deals that meet their requirements. Keeping your eye on the ball prevents you from chasing deals that aren't the right kinds of deals—and helps you avoid "shiny object syndrome," where every new opportunity becomes a distraction and a waste of time.

Rules of Thumb

Following are some general rules of thumb used by many real estate investors. Not all of them will work for you, or in every location every time. But having your own rules of thumb is important for quickly analyzing property deals and maximizing your results.

The Rule of Financial Intelligence

Recognizing the following definitions can help in decision making:

- Asset—puts money in your pocket
- Liability—takes money out of your pocket
- Good Debt—finances your assets, on which someone else makes the payments
- Bad Debt—finances your liabilities, which you make the payments on

The Rule of 72

This rule calculates how many years it will take you to double your money in an investment. Divide your annual rate of return by 72 to get the answer.

The 50 Percent Rule

The 50 percent rule assumes that non-mortgage expenses will eat up half of the income from a rental property each month. So, if your rental is bringing in $1,000 per month, expect maintenance and taxes and other expenses to cost you $500 per month.

The One Percent Rule

The one percent rule calls for investors to only look at income properties that can rent for at least one percent of the purchase price per month. So, if you are buying a $100,000 property, it should rent for at least $1,000 per month. Some investors set the benchmark even higher at 2 percent.

This, like the 50 percent rule, is a quick and dirty (QAD) calculation. When it comes to rental real estate, before you make any buying decision, use net operating income (NOI) calculations (see Chapter 22) for single-family properties and capitalization (CAP) rate for commercial properties.

Debt Service Ratio

Debt service ratio (DSR or DSCR) is normally used by commercial property lenders. This ratio compares annual mortgage payments to expected net operating income. Most lenders demand at least a ratio of 1.2, meaning your NOI is 20 percent more than your mortgage payments.

Confirming Property Values

Before you invest, or even figure out if a property is a good deal at a given price, you've got to know how much it is really worth.

Zillow Is for Suckers

Even though notoriously and often wildly inaccurate, Zillow's "Zestimates" continue to be used to guess the potential market value of properties by novice investors and sellers. The result is losses by sellers, who are led into falsely believing their properties are worth much more than they really are and then end up refusing viable offers. Online valuation tools too often rely on old data and simply can't accurately reflect the realities of your market.

BPO: The Broker's Price Opinion

Computer-generated valuations can't do what a set of human eyes can. In some instances, you may want a formal valuation analysis, called a broker's price opinion (BPO). A paid licensed professional visits the subject property, provides photographs, and prepares a full comparative market analysis. Providing your lender with accurate valuation information is critical to setting your loan in motion and securing good terms for your loan. A BPO does not replace an appraisal in most cases, but it's a good place to start when shopping lenders.

Property Tax Assessments

Property tax assessments can be a useful tool. But you need to understand how "inaccurate" they are in your market. For example, tax assessed value might typically be 25 percent lower than properties are currently trading for in a given county. Tax values may not reflect a newly gentrified area or any area experiencing environmental or other issues that negatively impact value. Time and experience in your market make it simpler, but in the meantime, go the next step and verify, verify, verify.

Comparable Market Analyses

Comparable market analyses (CMAs) are the presentation tools often used by real estate agents to guide homeowners in selecting a listing price. Realtors looking for listings will often prepare CMAs for free. Investors can also piece together their own by comparing the prices and features of recently sold properties, pending listings, and expired listings. This is essentially how appraisers start the evaluation of residential homes. However, it is an art, not a science, and it is always best to verify.

Automated Valuation Models

Automated valuation models (AVMs) are the next step up. They can sometimes be used in place of appraisals, but can be inaccurate. Of course, they are normally far cheaper and faster to obtain than full appraisals. Obtaining two of these AVMs to average out the findings can be helpful and empowers investors to move quickly and decisively.

Appraisals

Full appraisals are not cheap. You can't afford to order full appraisals on every prospective opportunity. Otherwise, you'll go broke before you do a deal. Your lenders will order their own appraisals and charge you for them, so it's a better alternative when initially evaluating a property to use the BPO or to develop relationships with local real estate agents. In any case, investors can move the loan process along and get better up-front answers by providing copies of previous valuations that give lenders all the specifics of a property along with photos.

Rent Verification

Verifying rents is a critical part of due diligence and accurately valuing rental real estate. If you get your rent estimates wrong, the true value of the property, how much your returns are, and how much you can borrow may be very different from initial expectations.

Never take figures offered by real estate agents and sellers at face value. Instead, ask for copies of rent rolls, do your own market research, and even test it out by running ads. Don't confuse asking rents with real rents, and make sure to understand different types of rental rates (e.g., weekly, annual, and Airbnb-type rentals).

Inspections

It's critical to do a preliminary walk-through and to obtain quotes from contractors. Once there is a contract in place, real property inspections should be ordered and completed immediately. This is when you find out just how ugly your baby really is. Way too many deals have been derailed by careless inspections that could have uncovered costly repairs, liens, and code restrictions on the property.

Is There a Lender for This Deal?

Before signing a contract or even making an offer, it pays to make sure there is a lender that funds your type of deal. While you aren't able to guarantee funding, you should have identified a lender whose criteria matches your deal. For example, there is no point making an offer on a property you hope to tear down and rebuild if there are no investment lenders that offer construction financing in your area for your property type. Do your screening, find a lender match, then forge ahead.

Finding the right lender means finding the right properties and doing your homework to get the deal closed. Carefully analyze the deal and the outcomes you expect—and don't be afraid to walk away from an ugly baby. Remember, not every deal is a good one.

TAKEAWAYS

- *There are a number of good ways to determine the value of a real property. Of the methods listed in this chapter, which can you employ in your business? Why are they the best choice?*
- *What are your basic criteria when looking for properties? This knowledge allows you to spend your time on the most viable opportunities.*

ESTIMATING
YOUR PROJECT'S COSTS

How Much Is Your Property Renovation Project Going to Cost?

As you're preparing to fund your deal, you'll need to have a good estimate of costs to bring the property up to marketable value. How can real estate investors properly estimate a project's expenses? What factors and steps are involved? What hidden issues do investors need to be wary of? How will the scope of work impact funding, and vice versa?

Knowing Your Customer and Your Exit Strategy

Before estimating rehab project costs, you should determine your exit strategy. Will you sell or hold it for a rental? Short term, mid-term, or long term? Whether it's a new development, a multifamily apartment building makeover, a single-family rehab, investors absolutely have to know their market and their customers.

What does the market demand in your area? You absolutely have to know what sells and rents in your area because that market demand should drive your renovation decisions and budget. New investors in particular need to pay attention to local market trends and not make renovation decisions based on their personal tastes.

Knowing your market and your end-buyer's "wish list" is the key to a project's success and acts as a guide for creating an effective and profitable scope of work and choosing the right materials. Ultimately, this knowledge helps investors to quickly and accurately assess a property and put together a funding request to lenders.

Inspecting and Evaluating the Property

After gaining experience from a number of rehab projects, investors should find that they are able to skillfully and very accurately sum up a property in thirty minutes or less. Even then, it always pays to double-check, verify, and investigate further with more thorough inspections. Property inspections and checklists are critical for staying organized, having clarity, and demonstrating value to lenders. Remember, lenders are looking to minimize risk and maximize returns and you should as well.

What types of inspections should real estate investors deploy? You have to remember, not all costs are related to things that are visible, or even related to the actual physical structure or land. Inspections include:

- Physical walk-throughs
- Professional third-party home inspections for residential property
- Environmental inspections for multifamily and commercial property
- Title and lien searches
- Final walk-through inspections before closing

If you cannot personally and physically walk the property or have one of your own trusted team members do it, then at a bare minimum you need to have a trusted local contact take and provide comprehensive photographs and videos of the property. Thorough, professional third-party inspections are always critical for digging in to identify repair needs, especially those lying under the surface. If you are not sure where to start with a preliminary inspection, it pays to bring along a more experienced investor, a trusted contractor, or a licensed inspector. New investors in particular need to rely on outside expertise to help them identify the "gotchas" that can turn a money maker into a money taker.

Don't overlook title and lien searches, either. They can reveal boundary issues and permitting and use issues, and may alert you to additional opportunities, as well as what you can and cannot do to a property. For example, if you are in a historic district or a homeowner association (HOA) community, you need to know because you may need to maintain certain design aspects in a renovation. In some areas, it's worthwhile to inquire at the local government office about code ordinances, development, infrastructure, former well sites, and other environmental issues that can impact your project.

General Rules of Thumb

Here are some of the common rules of thumb used when flipping houses and working the numbers on your property.

The 70 Percent Rule

The 70 percent rule demands that your acquisition and house renovation costs should not exceed 70 percent of the after-repair value (ARV) of a property. This issue is covered more thoroughly in Chapter 22.

Price per Square Foot (PSF)

In the case of fully gutted rehabs or additions, it can make sense to use local build costs per square foot to make sure you are on the safe side. If you plan to add a 1,000-square-foot home addition and build costs are around $100 per foot, estimate a $100,000 project cost.

Price per square foot is also useful for determining comparable values. Many areas use valuation models that are based on PSF.

Murphy's Law

Murphy is present on every fix and flip project. If something can go wrong, it probably will, and you must expect cost and time overages. This calculation calls for adding 20 percent more money and 80 percent more time to your estimates for completing a project. Somewhat tongue in cheek, this estimation tries to drive home the fact that your project will almost always take more money and time than you originally thought.

Obtaining Repair Estimates

Always obtain at least three repair estimates from different contractors until you have built reliable relationships. And always ask fellow investors for referrals. It's not uncommon in smaller markets for house flippers to use many of the same vendors.

Avoiding the Traps

There can be many pitfalls when taking on real estate projects. Here are four to watch out for.

Trap 1: Building Permits and Legal Use

Permit issues are one of the most financially catastrophic issues for newer investors. Minor building code violations such as overgrown landscaping may easily be overcome. But if you find out that a three-unit property is only legally a single-family dwelling, that will drastically change your figures. Some investors have even discovered a property is slated for demolition after they purchased it.

This illustrates why thorough due diligence is crucial, and why it also pays to have good relationships with local inspectors and local government in order to quickly vet properties and your plans for them prior to closing.

Trap 2: Capital-Draining Improvements

Understanding what actually adds tangible value to a property, and what doesn't, is one of the toughest things for new real estate investors to wrap their heads around. Not even all real estate agents understand this concept.

The first thing to recognize is the difference between boosting appeal versus actual appraised value. You can spend thousands of dollars on repairs and upfits and not get the return at resale. The pictures might look nicer and ads might get more clicks, but if the property doesn't appraise for more, buyers can't borrow any more to buy it. It all goes back to knowing your market and knowing your end-buyer.

Trap 3: What's Lurking Underneath?

What's underneath is usually the expensive stuff. It's those large, unexpected house remodeling costs that break the budget and timeline. And buyers can't even "see" the improvement as they can when it's a new kitchen or bath.

But those "hidden" repairs like roof structures, pest damage, and foundation repairs don't have to be deal breakers, if they are caught up front and accounted for in your repair estimates and purchase price. It is those sneaky plumbing or electrical problems, the rot under leaky siding, and other challenges hiding in the walls and under the floor that can turn a $5,000 rehab that should take thirty days to complete into a six-month, $50,000 or more money pit. Having a thorough inspector and contractors you can trust to point out potential issues in advance can be your best insurance.

Trap 4: What You Don't Inspect For

Not all of the big property killers are a part of the standard inspection list either. How about Chinese drywall and meth labs? Radon? Well testing? These factors can poison homes to such an extent that many ethical investors won't want to touch them, even if official remediation actions are taken. Know what issues are common in your area, and don't skimp on the relatively small costs to test for them.

In some cases, investors may have to pay renovation costs up front and then request disbursements from escrow. Do you have the liquidity to float these expenses? It's critical when choosing your funding to understand how you will access the funds throughout the renovation process.

Funding and the Numbers Game

Funding is a huge part of the numbers game. How much funding you can get will impact what repair and improvement items can be done, and to what level. Beyond the total funding amount, real estate investors need to pay attention to access to funds, and draws too.

Maximizing funding for real estate projects is also about knowing how to present your deal to prospective lenders. Your figures, executive summary, and presentation will reveal your true experience level. Optimize your presentation with subject-to appraisals and real contractor estimates, and avoid being unrealistically optimistic. Lenders work from numbers, not rose-colored glasses. Be prepared with real estimates, real comps, and realistic profitability projections.

The Scope of Work

All of your inspection work and desired improvements come together in the scope of work. This document lists all of the items that need to be done, what materials will be used, and deadlines.

If you are using just one contractor for the entire project, the contractor will likely provide the scope of work and estimated repair costs. If you will be doing some of your own work or will be directing several subcontractors yourself, you will want a master scope of work, in addition to contracts with each of your service providers.

Experienced rehabbers recommend leaving your scope of work at the property for contractors to review and bid on so that you ensure you are always comparing apples to apples. Keep it simple, so it's easy for all vendors to work with.

Tales from the Trenches

What can happen to a real estate investment when investors rush in, ignore common sense, and shortcut the inspection process?

What You Can't See

In one rehab, the flipper obtained an inspection but didn't do a walk-through, missing the fact that the outdated electrical system wouldn't even support a stove. The investor ended up completely tearing out the kitchen and bedroom walls, rewiring the house, and adding a new panel, which resulted in thousands of extra dollars in house renovation costs. Could the inspector be taken to task? Sure, but at a cost of both time and money—each critical to any renovation project. In another case, failure to properly test plumbing resulted in new tenants discovering exterior pipes had been destroyed by tree roots and sewage backing up in the house. This meant laying new exterior pipes and paying for tenants to stay somewhere else during the construction. These kinds of oversights are costly and can happen to anyone who lets exuberance override thorough due diligence.

Collaborating with Partners

If you've watched a couple of episodes of house-flipping shows on reality TV, you've already witnessed the challenges that can arise when renovating properties with partners. Sometimes the problems are worse than the stress of arguing over design finishes; partners can go as far as exceeding budgets and even borrowing against equity in the property to fund additional improvements. This can leave a property in a negative equity situation, meaning it cannot be resold without a loss. In one case, a partner took out a $30,000 line of credit against a property and spent it on personal items. The partner who put in over $30,000 in cash for improvements lost everything and the property went to foreclosure. Make sure there are clear boundaries for who is in charge of what. Chapter 9 covers partnerships in more detail.

Coordinating Contractors

One of the most common real estate investment blunders is failing to coordinate different contractors and phases of the job in the right order. For example, don't call in the drywaller before the electrician or plumber who needs access behind the walls. You don't want the next contractor to destroy the work of the previous one. Consider the order for doing plumbing, electrical work, floors, appliances, painting, ceilings, and other items.

Running Out of Money

Browse the internet and online real estate forums for fifteen minutes and you'll probably discover several real estate investment tales in which newbies failed to plan for overages and found they ran out of cash and had an unfinished property that could not be leased or sold. This is the fast path to bankruptcy. Always leave a cushion for additional expenses. Network with other investors to learn the realities of renovations, funding, and making a profit.

Seven Steps to Your Scope of Work

Accurately estimating project costs relies on thorough due diligence and inspections. To ensure plans are feasible, investors also need to take into account funding constraints and overages. This all comes together in a solid scope of work, which together with a little common sense and sound business practices will help investors to avoid the pitfalls.

Bringing it all together, this process can be summed up in seven steps.

1. Know your customer, local real estate market, and values.
2. Conduct thorough inspections as early as possible.
3. Get real quotes from licensed contractors.
4. Add in a time and money cushion for overages.
5. Prepare your detailed scope of work.
6. Re-run the numbers against values and anticipated funding.
7. Put your loan package together; provide the information your lender needs to make a quick decision.

TAKEAWAYS

- *What are biggest "gotchas" that can be discovered in a potential investment property? Include those found in this chapter plus any others that are common to your investment area.*
- *Before providing your lender with a loan package, ask yourself: "What information does the lender need to make a speedy decision?"*

THE TIME VALUE OF MONEY

Don't Underestimate the Value of Your Time

Have you ever heard the phrase, "Don't step over a dollar to pick up a dime?" This characterizes an often-made mistake of real estate investors.

In an effort to save cash and keep control, entrepreneurs will take on too much and rather than hire out the work, they try to do it all themselves. It's not uncommon for entrepreneurs to take on smaller, less business-critical tasks to "save money." They'll take on aspects of operations, managing customers and employees, and bringing in new business without help for getting the menial, routine tasks done. The end result? They spend time on minutiae rather than cash-generating, mission-critical activities (and suffer burnout from being pulled in a hundred different directions). The time value of money tells them to focus on the highest value activities to make the best use of their time. In situations like this, the entrepreneur could hire an assistant to tackle the routine tasks and instead spend time networking, traveling to trade shows, and focusing on business building and sustaining activities. Small-business owners who are smart will recognize how much money is being wasted doing everything themselves. Not time . . . but *money*.

 Tackling every task limits the mental and physical bandwidth of any individual to effectively focus on the more important aspects of their business (like cash-generating activities).

If you are a smart business owner you realize that the capacity to better develop and manage customer relationships will result in higher sales and better business outcomes—all because you're not bogged down in the more trivial aspects of running the business.

The same holds true for real estate investors. If you're a house flipper, are you really saving money painting that house yourself when that work could be hired out, leaving you free to do other, more critical cash-building things? More work gets done more quickly, the property goes to market faster, and you can do more deals than if you did all the work yourself.

The lesson here? *Don't step over dollars to save dimes.*

So now that you understand the real cost of stepping over dollars for dimes and the importance of seriously analyzing where you invest your time in your business, let's take a look at a concept that too many investors ignore. It's ignored because many people don't know about it.

The Time Value of Money

At its most basic, the time value of money is the notion that money today is worth more than money tomorrow.

Why Money Has Time Value

First of all, why does money have time value? The time value of money is the economic principle that a dollar received today has greater value than a dollar received in the future. The idea behind this concept is easy to see with a simple example. Suppose you were given the choice between receiving $100,000 today or $100,000 in 100 years. Which option would you rather take? Clearly $100,000 today is more valuable for the following reasons:

- No Risk. There is no risk of having to get money back that you already have today.
- Higher Purchasing Power. Because of inflation, $100,000 can be exchanged for more goods and services today than $100,000 can in 100 years. Put another way, just think back to what $100,000 could buy you 100 years ago. That $100,000 in 1917 would be the equivalent of roughly $2.3 million today.
- Opportunity Cost. A dollar received today can be invested now to earn interest, resulting in a higher value in the future. In contrast, a dollar received in the future cannot begin earning interest until it is received. This lost opportunity to earn interest is the opportunity cost.

Combined, these concepts should drive investors looking to build a viable, long-term wealth-building business to really consider carefully how they use their time, skills, and vision as a driving force.

Opportunity Costs = The Money Value of Your Time

The Time Value of Money = The Opportunities Today and Tomorrow

TAKEAWAYS

- *Think about your "cash-generating activities." What are they in your business?*
- *Now that you've identified the best value-add activities, what can you do to stay focused on them versus investing time in other tasks that can easily be hired out?*

22

WHAT EVERY INVESTOR NEEDS TO KNOW ABOUT TERMS, CASH FLOW, AND FORMULAS

Do You Know What You Don't Know?

Before you even approach a lender, you have to know the terms of engagement, so to speak. Though you may have purchased a house before, real estate investing is the polar opposite of buying a personal home. Investing is all about the numbers; buying a personal residence is a more emotional undertaking. Sound real estate investment is based on knowing and using tried-and-true formulas and principles.

 For real estate investors to succeed, they must know, understand, and use a basic set of formulas to guide their decision making—all based on the numbers.

MAO or the 70 Percent Rule

Used by house flippers, The maximum allowable offer (MAO) formula is based on the 70 percent rule. The 70 percent rule is the notion that an investor cannot pay more than 70 percent of the after-repair value (ARV) of the property after accounting for the cost of your funding, repairs, holding costs, and resale commissions and costs.

The 70 percent rule works as shown in Table 22-1.

Table 22-1.
The 70 percent rule for maximum allowable offer (MAO).

ARV	$150,000	Value of property after repairs
Loan (Cost of Funding)	– 6,000	Origination fees, closing fees, interest
Repairs	– 25,000	All expenses related to renovations
Holding Costs	– 2,000	Insurance, utilities, taxes, HOA, other
Resale Fees	– 9,000	Realtor fees (6%)
MAO Rule Applied	= $108,000 × 0.70	ARV minus costs to flip Multiplied by 0.70
Max Allowable Offer	= $ 75,600	

If it all plays out as planned, your profit is $32,400 ($108,000 – $75,600), which represents the total expenses minus the purchase price or MAO.

When is it okay to break the 70 percent rule?

- When you have a guaranteed built-in buyer, so there's no need to pay resale fees.
- When your cost of money is lower (e.g., a subject-to transaction) or you have access to cheap cash

The Wholesaler's Formulas

Wholesalers use the same basic formula but include a wholesale fee that is determined in one of two ways: a percentage formula or a set-fee formula.

The 65 Percent Rule

They use a 65 percent rule to account for their fee, where:

ARV – Costs to Flip × 0.65 = Max Offer When Wholesaling

Using the example in Table 22-1, the wholesaler would make an offer of $70,200 to the seller and charge the investor-buyer a $5,400 wholesale fee—which is the difference between a 70 percent and 65 percent MAO.

$108,000 × 0.70 = $75,600 (70% Rule)

$108,000 × 0.65 = $70,200 (65% Rule)

$75,600 – $70,200 = $5,400 (Wholesale Fee)

The Set-Fee Formula

Wholesalers also use a set-fee amount. Using the same example as Table 22-1, the wholesaler adds the fee into the costs to flip. Let's say this wholesaler wanted a bigger fee because it was a difficult property to get under contract. The formula would look something like the one shown in Table 22-2.

Table 22-2. **The wholesale set-fee formula**

ARV	$150,000	Value of property after repairs
Loan (Cost of Funding)	– 6,000	Origination fees, closing fees, interest
Repairs	– 25,000	All expenses related to renovations
Holding Costs	– 2,000	Insurance, utilities, taxes, HOA, other
Resale Fees	– 9,000	Realtor fees (6%)
MAO Rule Applied	= $108,000 × 0.70	ARV minus costs to flip Multiplied by .70
70% Rule Applied Minus Wholesale Fee	= $75,600 – $10,000	Net BEFORE wholesale fee
Max Allowable Offer	$ 65,600	

An Alternative to the 70 Percent Rule for Flippers

Every property that is fixed and flipped requires a different amount of time and cash and has different considerations. The 70 percent rule, at its most basic, builds in a 30 percent profit margin and can be a great rule of thumb.

But investors can also look at a property that may be a quick and easy flip and decide that the property is a good deal even if doesn't meet the 70 percent rule—simply because the time and money needed to complete the deal is less effort.

The Desired Profit Formula

Rather than use a margin, use a set profit amount. For example, let's say you can pick up a 1,000-square-foot brick ranch in a very marketable neighborhood. The ARV is $150,000. The house only needs some basic cosmetics to bring it up to market, and you can get the job done with little time and hassle. Repair costs are only $12,000, and holding costs are lower because the renovation time is shorter.

In this case, you'll build in your desired profit (dollar amount) to determine your offer (see Table 22-3).

Table 22-3. **The desired profit formula for flipping.**

ARV	$150,000	Value of property after repairs
Loan (Cost of Funding)	– 5,000	Origination fees, closing fees, interest
Repairs	– 12,000	All expenses related to renovations
Holding Costs	– 1,000	Insurance, utilities, taxes, HOA, other
Resale Fees	– 9,000	Realtor fees (6%)
Desired Profit	= $123,000 – 20,000	ARV minus costs to flip
Max Allowable Offer	= $103,000	

Net Operating Income

Investors looking for cash flow and the benefits of building wealth through more passive rental income use the net operating income (NOI) formula for determining how much financial leverage makes sense.

Rental properties should support themselves. The conservative investor will never over-leverage into a position of negative cash flow. NOI takes into consideration the expenses you have *today*—although it is important to remember that rents rise over time, as do expenses.

Tables 22-4 and 22-5 show you the basic gross operating income and net operating income formulas to use when considering purchasing or refinancing a rental property. The formulas are based on monthly numbers: rent minus expenses equals cash flow (excluding mortgage payments).

Table 22-4. **Gross income for rentals.**

Rent	$1,000	
Taxes	−150	
Insurance	−75	
Vacancy (10%)	−100	Can vary with turnover rate
Repairs (8%)	−80	Varies by property but helps you budget for repairs
Management (10%)	−100	Payment to yourself, even if you self-manage
Gross Operating Income	$495	Monthly income BEFORE any debt payment (mortgage)

The gross operating income tells you how much mortgage the rental property can support today. While some investors own rental properties free and clear, many others don't. You can use any mortgage calculator to determine how much loan makes sense when funding a rental property when you know the gross rental income.

In this case, the property could support a payment up to $495. So working backward using a mortgage calculator to get to a payment close to $495, you can determine that this property can support a mortgage of around $92,000 for thirty years at 5 percent, for a payment of $493.88.

Gross Operating Income $495 − $493.88 = $1.12 Monthly Cash Flow

It's important to understand that this example does not result in significant cash flow today. The conservative investor might run the numbers using an NOI formula to include cash flow from day one (see Table 22-5).

Table 22-5. **Net operating income for rentals.**

Rent	$1,000	
Taxes	−150	
Insurance	−75	
Vacancy (10%)	−100	Can vary with turnover rate
Repairs (8%)	−80	Varies by property but helps you budget for repairs
Management (10%)	−100	Payment to yourself, even if you self-manage
Gross Operating Income	$495	Monthly income BEFORE any debt payment (mortgage)
Desired Cash Flow	−100	
Net Operating Income	$395	Amount of monthly debt payment the property can support while paying operating expenses and cash flow

With cash flow now built into your numbers, you can use a mortgage calculator to determine how much mortgage the property can support with a loan payment of $395.

There are a multitude of terms, formulas, and strategies that make for sound investing; what I've outlined here for you are just a few examples. Commercial investors use capitalization (CAP) rate for multifamily properties. Cash-on-cash calculations help investors compare returns for the use of their available cash. Following these principles and knowing your numbers will keep you from making "feel good" decisions and keep your business strong.

TAKEAWAYS

- *When should you use alternatives to the basic 70 percent rule?*
- *Why does it make sense to use net operating income when determining the financials on a rental property?*

23

THE HOLE POKER

The Devil's Advocate

An Important Part of Your Real Estate Investment Team

What is a "hole poker" and why should all real estate investors consider having one?

It's far too easy for real estate investors to get blinded by their optimism and eagerness to steam forward, ignore the formulas, and make mistakes. Others may give up too quickly when a deal looks tough to negotiate. So how can a hole poker help? Where can you find one? And are there cases when you should ignore a hole poker?

Emotional vs. Fact-Based Real Estate Investment

Chapter 19 ("Is Your Baby Ugly?") offered insights into looking closely at your investment. Is your deal really a deal, and will a lender fund it? Both new and experienced real estate investors can let their emotions get the better of them when presented with new opportunities.

We buy real estate for many different reasons. And while there is absolutely a personal side to real estate, as Warren Buffett says, "Investment is best when most businesslike." This means investing based on facts, not emotions.

This is also where a hole poker comes in. This is someone who serves as a devil's advocate of sorts, whose goal is to poke holes in your deal. A good hole poker should consider all aspects of your deal:

- Is the location good?
- Is the price right?
- Does the funding model support the exit strategy?
- Is the exit strategy sound and viable?
- Do the numbers work, and have the right formulas and calculations been used?
- Can the necessary repairs be completed on budget?
- Is it reasonable to expect the repairs to be completed on time? Is labor readily available?

These are some of the questions a good hole poker should ask . . . and help answer.

Sometimes aspiring investors get frustrated and give up too easily. They allow inexperience and impatience to take money right out of their pockets, instead of making the extra couple of calls needed to get the deal done right. The truth is, you might have to try several lenders to get your deal financed, but when there are tens or hundreds of thousands of dollars or more on the line it is usually worth it, and an extra set of eyes can only be helpful in averting problems.

Other investors let optimism and bullishness override the facts, which causes them to neglect commonsense investment principles, like using proven formulas and practicing due diligence. This is a major threat to sustainable investing. In severe cases, it can lead to very heavy losses. Bullishness played a big part in the derailment of the property market in the early 2000s.

It's absolutely vital to invest by the facts. Once you've done your due diligence, it's time to check your facts.

The Value of Second Opinions for Funding

There's a good reason that patients get a second opinion before undergoing major surgery. There can be big risks. Are there alternatives and what are they? When it comes to real estate, there can be big risks to your financial health, especially when there are oversights and careless blunders. So, it only makes sense to get second opinions on your investments, too. After all, your finances are your lifeline.

When it comes to closing deals for funding, get a second opinion on:

- Purchase contract terms
- Loan terms, timelines, and other stipulations
- Results of the appraisal
- Manageability of the timelines and scope of work
- Viability of your exit strategy

These are all important considerations when navigating the funding phase of your deal. Getting feedback on these individual items can often save investors thousands of dollars and a tremendous amount of time.

The Hole Poker

As the title suggests, the hole poker's job is to intentionally poke holes in your big-picture plans and your individual deals. When you've got a real estate deal on the table, and maybe even before that, when you are formulating an investment plan or business plan, it pays to get that second opinion and to ask, "Can you find a problem with this?"

Ask:

- Is this a good deal and how can I make it happen?
- What issues or potential pitfalls do you see in my plan?

- Have you done a deal like this, and what did you learn from it?
- Do my estimates and assumptions look accurate?
- Is this a good use of my time, credit, and dollars?
- How can I make this deal even better and more profitable?
- Would you do this deal, and if so, how would you make it happen?

Where to Find a Good Hole Poker

If you were buying your first car, you'd probably take someone who knows cars along with you—someone who knows where to look under the hood for issues and knows how to negotiate better deals. Most of us at least have an experienced car buyer in our family somewhere, maybe even a mechanic. But far fewer people may have a true real estate investment expert to turn to. So where can you find a good and trusted advocate to help you reduce risk and maximize profits?

Certain people may make good hole pokers, including:

- Real estate attorneys
- Financial planners who understand real estate investing
- Real estate investment coaches
- Other real estate investors from your social network or from the local Real Estate Investors Association (REIA)
- Your private money lenders
- Trusted contractors

The point is to find people with more experience, who have proved their ability to successfully navigate the market, and whose input you can trust. Not all hole pokers can assess every aspect of your deal. You may want an attorney to pick apart your purchase contract and loan terms. You get the idea. If you can't find an all-in-one adviser, don't be afraid to ask for the opinion of different experts.

How to Get a Great Hole Poker to Help You

How do you get someone with far more experience, who can often earn hundreds of dollars an hour, to give you their feedback? Hiring them is the most obvious answer. Most of the time they'll more than pay for themselves by offering a few tips on how to improve the deal or telling you to back away from a bad deal, but if you can't afford it, there are other options. Find places they hang out and network. Local real estate investor groups or professional group meetings are a great place. If you have a business relationship with some of these professionals already, take them to lunch or for a coffee. They might start asking to do business with you as a private money lender or partner.

Knowing When to Go Your Own Way

Sometimes, despite the advice of others, you've still got to go your own way. Sometimes you'll see what others don't. It may be an opportunity they don't understand and you just have to go with your gut. Perhaps their understanding of your big-picture goals is unclear; perhaps they don't understand the market, the property, or the remedies you can employ.

That's okay too—but do so with caution and a clear understanding of why and how your approach makes more sense than the input of others. Often, that's how new progress is made and uncommon returns are obtained. But beware: It can also go exactly the opposite. For a safe investment, base your decision on reality, not speculation.

When you use a hole poker, at least you'll be keenly aware of the facts and alert to the potential pitfalls. It's wise to use a hole poker on your deals. Just make sure your hole poker has credibility, experience, and a track record of success, and that it is someone whose advice you can trust, so every deal can be a good deal, no matter what advice you decide to act on.

TAKEAWAYS

- *Think of the people already in your network and what role(s) they can play in examining the financials of your deal. Who in your network could you call on to examine your deal?*
- *Who would make a good "hole poker" for looking at your funding?*
- *Why does it make sense to use others to poke holes in your deal when it comes to the property, the market, the scope of work, and aspects of your deal other than funding?*

NEXT! KNOW WHEN TO WALK AWAY FROM A REAL ESTATE DEAL

The Bite Test

When should real estate investors walk away from a potential deal?

Not every shiny gold-colored object is valuable. Fool's gold and fake gold can appear almost identical to the real thing. So can counterfeit $100 bills. That's why we've all heard of the "bite test" to check for real gold and why stores have special lights, pens, and identifiers to spot counterfeit money.

There are a lot of potential real estate deals out there that aren't the real deal either. Even dirt-cheap homes selling for $1,000 can turn out to be duds. And even brand-new shiny oceanfront penthouses selling for millions of dollars can be terrible deals in disguise. And more often than not, nothing is a deal unless you can land the right funding.

 In real estate, the bite test is due diligence. And every deal should take you closer to your big-picture goals and meet your criteria for profitability.

The whole point of investing in real estate is to make the most of your money and time. So you simply can't afford to burn resources taking big risks on properties that perform poorly. Each one needs to pass the bite test. And in many cases, you want to get a second opinion from a trusted "hole poker" (see Chapter 23) who will keep you in check.

When should investors walk away from a potential deal?

There are a number of reasons to pass on a property, and the earlier investors toss it back in the stream, the sooner they turn their attention to finding the real gold. Here are a few scenarios:

- The deal doesn't directly help achieve your larger goals.
- You are unable to perform thorough due diligence.
- Financing costs put you at risk or diminish returns too steeply.
- Risks are too high.
- Profit potential is purely based on speculation.
- The numbers change for the worse.
- You lack the experience or resources for the asset class or property type.
- The property has some sort of oddity or pitfall that can make it hard to sell.

If physical inspections aren't possible and contractor estimates or title insurance can't be secured, you're just asking for the worst-case scenario by moving ahead. To ignore the results of your due diligence, or skip it altogether, can get unbelievably expensive. If the numbers are too thin at the beginning, they are only likely to get thinner later. That can mean negative cash flow or having to pay money to get rid of a liability. That's no fun, and it certainly breaks Warren Buffett's golden rule: "Don't lose money."

Surprises can happen at closing, too. Sorry to say, there are some bad lenders out there—and they will count on you not walking away from your deal. They may try to up their fees or change the terms at the last minute. Bad financing from any lender, reputable or not, can break a good deal. That extra thousand or two can rob you of cash flow or force you to make a bad renovation decision. Sometimes you just have to walk away.

In other cases, sellers will refuse to permit the walkthrough before closing, or an occupant isn't out. This presents massive legal and financial risks that most people can't afford to take. There may be times when you have to bite the bullet on a few thousand dollars in expenses already accrued, but that's likely better than taking on thousands of dollars in bad liabilities.

Taking a Hit

If real estate investors make enough offers and do enough deals, eventually most of them end up taking some hits. You can be a great boxer, but if you get in the ring enough times someone is eventually going to get a punch in, or even beat you. That's only career ending if you give up, stay down, throw in the towel, and retire. On the other hand, if you get back up, get more punches than you take, and win more than you lose, you can still win in the real estate game for a long time. The key is minimizing those income hits. Sometimes it is a matter of blocking. Other times it is stepping into the swing, to intercept the punch early, to take the power out of the hit.

Performing as much due diligence as early as you can, having strong contracts and a good corner person (e.g., attorney, coach, or hole poker), and knowing when not to throw good money after bad are all ways to minimize damage. You may occasionally have to walk away from earnest money deposits and money invested in due diligence. That's a cost of doing business. Don't let it ruin your mindset. Learn from it, adjust your game, do better next time. It's a lot better to take a little jab and bruise to the ego than to get knocked flat out of the ring.

Living to Fight Another Day

Truly wealthy investors often make investment moves that seem overly cautious to new real estate investors. Why? Seasoned investors "live to fight another day." If you are still in the game, not over-leveraged and not speculating, you can always make a comeback even after a stumble. In real estate investing, this means preserving your capital and credit to make further investments.

So invest your time in due diligence up front, and don't take a bad deal just for the sake of doing a deal. Act decisively and wisely, working with facts, not emotions and misguided hope. The real heavy hitters are the leading investors who differentiate themselves by being able to act quickly and decisively—and it's all based on facts. It is said that the best decision you can make is the best choice; the second best is just to make a decision.

Plenty of Fish in the Sea

You must know when to walk away from a bad real estate deal, and be willing to do so. And just as important, know that there are more deals out there. Don't do deals just for the sake of doing a deal. Do it for realizing profits and building wealth. There's another house and another deal just around the corner.

TAKEAWAYS

- *List all the reasons that would prompt you personally to walk away from a potential deal. What are your deal breakers?*

25

DEALING WITH DETOURS

The Power of Plan B

It doesn't matter what business you are in, it's always smart to have a Plan B. If there's one thing that's certain in life and in real estate, it's that things change. Your goals may change, market and neighborhood dynamics can change, and unforeseen events can put your plans into a complete 180.

Savvy real estate investors love deals that have multiple potential exit strategies. Lenders love when they pledge capital to fund a project that has multiple exit strategies. It dramatically reduces risk and increases odds of success.

What are your exit strategies and alternate options in case you can't flip that house on the schedule you planned? Or what if that long-term hold is impacted by outside factors? What detours can you consider to minimize the downside of the deal?

Ten Detours to Take When Things Don't Go as Planned

1. Wholesale the property as-is.
2. Clean it out and sell it as a handyman special.
3. Bring in a partner.

4. Rent instead of selling it.
5. Lease it out short term, via Airbnb.
6. Convert condos to rentals, or rentals to condos.
7. Renovate instead of wholesaling it.
8. Offer seller financing or lease options.
9. Rezone the property to match the highest and best use.
10. Refinance.

Important Considerations for a Successful Venture

Consider where you really want your real estate investing to take you. Even when faced with a detour, real property is an asset—especially when it's funded correctly. Every property requires the right amount of time, skills, and funding to be successful. Map out your Plan A. Where do you want the property to take you (in terms of short- or long-term profits) and how do you want to get there (the best exit strategy)? Consider the potential detours you could face and then consider alternative routes. Different strategies get different results, and the steps for each may be very different—but being prepared for twists and turns will make you a more nimble investor who can take advantage of multiple opportunities.

TAKEAWAYS

- *What are some alternatives when a fix and flip takes a wrong turn?*
- *How can you remedy a rental that isn't performing?*

WHAT COMES FIRST?
THE DEAL OR THE DOLLARS?

Getting Ready to Be Ready

When it comes to real estate investment, funding is like your fuel. Funding keeps the deals going, whether it's fix and flip projects or long-term holds for passive income. It pays to make sure you have not only enough funding but also the right kind of funding to keep all your investment activities on track.

> Do you need funding first or a signed purchase agreement? Do you need to have financing to make offers and cut deals? Or do you need a solid deal and exit strategy to get a loan lined up?

Putting the Horse Before the Cart

It's the proverbial chicken and egg of real estate investment. So, which needs to come first? In short, it depends.

Confusing, right? The truth is that you need a little of both. Some real estate agents and sellers won't even speak with you, never mind actually show you a property, unless you have proof of funds to purchase or are at least equipped with a mortgage preapproval letter. At the same time it is difficult for lenders to give you a solid loan commitment with terms that will stick unless they know the details of the transaction.

And when working with asset-based lenders, where the funding is based on the asset rather than the borrower, it gets even stickier.

 Lenders are used to providing preliminary funding letters for making offers. If you are using a private money lender, you can get documentation from them. It all depends on what the seller and lender require.

The best way forward is to obtain a preliminary mortgage funding approval based on your financial information and general scenario. Start talking with lenders, learn their funding criteria, and get a list of documentation requirements so that you can act quickly.

Once you have at least a preliminary funding plan in place, then you can go out and make competitive offers with confidence. Once you have a signed contract, then you go back to your lender with all of the specifics, get the loan underwritten, and obtain a solid funding commitment.

So find several funding sources and start the process—but before you do, remember these key points.

Finding the Right Funding Sources for Your Deals

If funding is like the fuel for your real estate deals, it's important to pick the right kind of fuel. Putting short-term funding on a property that you hold long term can destroy your investment vehicle and your returns.

There are different funding sources specializing in different types of financing. Short-term, long-term, income-based, equity-based—there are lots of different funding options. You have to go to the right lender to get the right fuel for your real estate investment based on where you plan to take it. For example, if you walk into a bank and say you want a loan with no credit check to buy a distressed property, and oh, you want money to fix it up too, what do think will happen? Most likely they'll smile and show you the door. Take the same deal somewhere else—to an asset-based lender (i.e., the right kind of lender)—and that lender might work aggressively to help you close the deal.

How do you know what kind of lender will meet your needs? It depends on your plans for the property and how long you need the money in play.

- **Short-Term Funding.** A lot of house flippers use what is often called hard money, where the loan terms are usually less than one year and typically come with higher rates and fees. Easier to qualify for, they are usually entirely asset-based, which means the loan is qualified based on the property, not on the borrower (you). The higher cost of borrowing is calculated into the deal. If the numbers work, this type of funding can be a good option. Short-term funding is used for all kinds of properties (e.g., single family, multi-units, commercial and land deals) and is often used to bridge the funding from the initial acquisition into more permanent financing.

- **Mid-Term Funding.** This is great for properties you sell on a lease option or plan to hold as a rental for eight or ten years or less. Some commercial lenders and many private money lenders prefer to fund these types of properties. They get better-than-market interest rates but don't charge as much as a hard money lender. Their investment is secured by an income-producing asset and they earn secured, steady interest income. The loan can have an adjustable rate for part of the term and/or a balloon payment.

■ **Long-Term Funding.** If you plan to hold a property for the long run, then you need long-term financing sources. Federal Housing Administration (FHA) lending guidelines seem to change every six months, and for the real estate investor, securing multiple loans for single-family properties can be a wild goose chase if you look for conventional funding. But it is possible to find a reliable funding source—typically a local portfolio lender. For multifamily and commercial properties, long-term funding is based on the property's income and capacity to generate cash flow. Be aware, however, that funding for commercial properties (including some multifamily) is typically based on a twenty-year amortization versus thirty years for single-family residential mortgage options.

Regardless of your source of funding, make sure the property and the plans you have for it are supported by a solid plan for the financing. Having a loan called due when you don't have a good exit laid out is a certain fast track to major setbacks and even failure.

What You Need to Get Going

Depending on the type of transaction you are working, you may need:

- Deposit money
- Funds to cover due diligence
- Proof-of-funds letters
- Closing costs
- Renovation and upfit money

You may also need to plan enough cash and credit to cover holding costs, marketing, and a cushion for reserves. Balloon loans and adjustable rate mortgages can be popular in some niches, but proceed with caution on these types of loans. A balloon payment on a loan when an investor is not prepared to pay it off can immediately steer you off course and turn a great property into a train wreck.

Funding really is like fuel for an investor, and just like any road trip, give yourself enough gas in case of detours or delays. They will happen. In these situations, it may be worth exploring single-close construction to permanent loans, or mini-perms, as well as flexible credit lines based on your overall portfolio equity and net worth.

Longevity as an investor requires making informed choices about funding sources, funding types, and the right funding applied to the right property and situation. Funding is the fuel that can propel an investor forward, but if used haphazardly, it can have the opposite effect. Develop relationships with private lenders, get to know funding sources for your property types, and go into each deal with a solid plan for capital to underpin the property and project.

TAKEAWAYS

- *This chapter identified five things you need to get going. Of those, which do you have?*
- *Now, list the things you don't have and what steps you can take to get them.*

27

PREPARING TO GET YOUR LOAN FUNDED

Failing to Plan Is Planning to Fail

You've located a great property, run the numbers, and completed your due diligence. You've decided to go it alone or bring in a partner; you've sourced your down payment. Now it's time to get your deal funded.

We all know the saying: "Failing to plan is planning to fail." This is never truer than when it comes to getting a real estate deal funded.

Planning for Success

What steps do real estate investors need to take in order to be prepared to successfully and expediently get funded? Let's start with a broad overview, then dig into the details.

1. Know what you'll need to fund your deal.
2. Know the forms you'll be expected to sign and what they mean.
3. Anticipate what your lender may demand.
4. Understand the common issues, and how to stay ahead of them.

What You Need to Fund Your Deal

Each lender and loan scenario will have specific criteria and demands, but there are essentials that will apply to every loan. They include:

- Valid ID for closing the loan
- Social Security or tax ID number
- Valid real estate contract (for purchases)
- Insurable title
- Title insurance (with lender mortgagee clause)
- Property insurance

And last but never least, especially in the eyes of the lender, is *cash*. Lenders require that you have "skin in the game," and for the most part the notion of "no money down" is merely a way of saying none of *your* money down. (How to secure a down payment is covered in Chapter 14.)

Depending on the property type, the loan, and the lender, some typical items that may be required include:

- Credit checks
- Property appraisals
- Income verification or rent rolls
- Scope of work and budgets for remodels and upfits
- Asset verification

Lenders won't ask for all of this documentation up-front, but the more you can provide earlier, the smoother the process will be, with fewer unpleasant surprises along the way. While it is often tempting to go the route requiring the least documentation (which can sometimes be best), it can also pay to provide more information in exchange for better rates and terms.

Mortgage Forms and Documents

What are the most important forms and documents real estate investors will encounter in the process of getting financing?

Loan Applications

The form real estate loan applications take can vary widely depending on the lender and type of loan being applied for. It may be the standard Fannie Mae residential home application. It could be a short online form, or lenders may expect borrowers to lead in with an executive summary.

An executive summary is a simple two- to three-page document that outlines the opportunity, who's involved in the execution of the deal, and the loan request. A good executive summary should include:

- Property details: description, market conditions, as-is and after-repair value (ARV) projections
- Transaction details
- Profile of the principals and management team
- Project description: acquisition and exit, anticipated returns, how it will be executed
- Loan request: terms and plans for servicing debt

For your loan application, lay out all the specifics of the transaction and as much personal or business financial information as is required by the lender for the specific loan program.

Scope of Work

If there are repairs, renovations, or construction work involved, your scope of work will play a significant role in moving your loan forward. Both lenders and appraisers will use this document to assess the ultimate value of the property, how much to loan, and when. Make sure this document is thorough, accurate, and realistic.

Closing Documents

The closing documents are the most important in the whole process today. The previously mentioned documents may dictate whether you will make it to the closing, but don't underestimate this last part of the real estate transaction.

Closing documents lay out the final terms of your loan and transaction. That means how much you need to close, the interest rate, payments, loan term, and more. This collection of documents also includes a hefty variety of disclosures. As mind-numbing and time-consuming as closing may be, read all of the fine print and ask questions until you get it. Do not sign anything unless it is 100 percent accurate. This is where having a solid relationship with your closing attorney or title office is critical.

Quick Tips for Setting Up a Smooth Funding Process

- Read your forms and documents in advance until you are comfortable with them.
- Request a funding checklist of all the items your lender needs to close.
- Anticipate potential lender demands and have the paperwork ready.
- Return requested documents ASAP.
- Get due diligence items completed immediately.

- Appoint someone to manage the transaction (e.g., realtor, mortgage broker, assistant).
- Agree on updates and timelines in advance so that you aren't panicking or slowing down the process with nonstop calls and messages.
- Focus on developing relationships with lenders who are excited about doing business with you and will facilitate an easy process for repeat deals.

The more you are prepared with knowledge going in, the smoother your venture will go. Be ready with the paperwork you need, and watch all the fine print. Then set up a process that will ensure speedy progress to real estate closing after closing. Once you've closed a few transactions, the process becomes less intimidating and you'll have a foundation for setting yourself up for success.

🏠 TAKEAWAYS

- *Make a list of everything you need to close a loan.*
- *Request a checklist and timeline from your potential lenders.*

WHO TO TAKE WITH YOU

The Real Estate Professionals You Need to Close the Deal

Who are the real estate professionals most investors need to get their deals closed? Whether it's locating investment-quality properties or closing the deal, the team you surround yourself with is an important part of your business.

They say your network is your net worth, and this is especially true in real estate investing.

Seven Real Estate Pros to Have on Your Side

Realtors

Some see it as a competitive relationship, but many real estate agents and investors have discovered the benefits of working together.

Realtors now realize that investors buy multiple properties, and they buy properties that most other buyers don't want. And investors realize that brokers have access to networks, relationships, and information that is of mutual benefit. Real estate may be seen as a "properties business," but when the rubber hits the road, it's a people business.

Mortgage Professionals and Private Money Lenders

Just as important is the relationship you build with potential lenders. Nearly every aspect of real estate investing is relationship based, so the more relationships you can build with those with capital to invest, the better. Even if you are sourcing real estate investment capital and mortgage loans online, relationships matter. The team involved, the individuals you communicate with, and the processors who work your files are essential to your success.

To streamline your loan requests to closing and get those difficult deals past quirky underwriting processes, you'll need a skilled loan officer who will go the extra mile for you to ensure easy processing, on-time closings, and great deals, again and again. When it comes to private money lenders, the relationship is typically built prior to ever putting a funding request in front of them, but that's not always the case. Regardless, investors are well served to build these connections and treat their funding relationships with the utmost care.

Title Company Reps

Title searches are a key part of real estate and protect you in the event of some sort of cloud on the title. Your title company rep is more than just a salesperson or someone you hire to do research. Title companies are a gateway to many auxiliary services. Build a good relationship here, so they go the extra mile in resolving title issues before they threaten to derail your deals. Title company reps can also offer you property leads, help make the numbers work at closing, and connect you with real estate attorneys for help in negotiating liens, contract terms, and other items.

Insurance Agents

Insurance may be about as much fun as taxes, but it is one of those must-haves. A good insurance contact will help minimize premiums, maximize coverage, and sometimes most important, get the work done fast so you can close. Investors are well served to work with agents experienced in rentals, rehab projects, and commercial property. It pays to network with other investors and find out who they use for each property type.

Real Estate Attorneys

A real estate attorney is an essential member of any real estate investor's team. Contract issues will happen, deposit disputes will arise, tenant problems will come up—the list of "could happens" is exhaustive. Every investor must develop a relationship with a local attorney to help navigate the legal waters of investment real estate. If you don't know a credible real estate attorney, trust that your fellow investors and local Real Estate Investors Association (REIA) do. Ask for referrals rather than simply relying on a web search. This is an important relationship and you want someone who knows the ropes of investment real estate.

Inspectors

Some investors do their own property inspections because their years of experience have made a basic inspection fairly routine. But there are situations that require the services of a licensed inspector.

If you are a new investor, you can learn a tremendous amount from an inspector. Look for one who will welcome your presence during the inspection (not all inspectors do, so developing that relationship is important). Overall, inspector relationships can be even more important in certain cases due to the short inspection period. You may have thirty to forty-five days to close, but only three to ten days to inspect the property and negotiate repairs or request your deposit money back. If you can't get an inspector out in that time frame, a lot of money and other relationships can be on the line. Then, of course, there is the need for accurate evaluations of acquisitions, too. And you may have more than one inspector relationship. You may need a basic home inspector for single-family properties, another capable of environment inspections on commercial properties, and good contacts for getting inspections passed on renovation and building projects.

Closers: The Paralegals

Many people agree that closers are often the most vital yet most undervalued professional in the real estate transaction. Sometimes the closer will also be your title company rep, but not always. Your closer may also work for your real estate attorney and is often a paralegal. The closer works to ensure the deal gets closed on time, even if all the realtors, mortgage company contacts, and others are unreachable.

Depending on the nature of your real estate investment business, you will need a variety of team members to make your mission a reality. As you choose the people you want to work with, be cautious: Get referrals, take the time to vet them, and look for those whose work style matches your own. Building a quality team can take time and you should expect it to be a process of trial and error, but in the end, the time and effort are a great payoff.

TAKEAWAYS

- *Start building your team now. Make a list of each of the professionals identified in this chapter. Beside each, list either:*
  - A professional already in your networkb.
  - Someone who can provide you with a referral

29

ESTIMATING YOUR TIME OF ARRIVAL

How Long Does It Take to Fund and Close a Real Estate Deal? And What Can Real Estate Investors Do to Streamline the Process?

Real estate closings and, in particular, financed acquisitions can be tricky. Yet, being able to count on a closing is crucial for real estate investors who want to keep consistent deal flow and a solid reputation. So how can investors successfully navigate the common roadblocks?

How Long Will It Take to Close?

Before digging into this question, it helps to go back and remember the big-picture real estate investing game plan. Real estate investment, like wealth building in general, is a marathon, not a sprint. Each deal should fit in and propel you toward your overall mission. But there will be moments to sprint—and closings are often sprint time.

You want to be able to make offers fast, close fast, and resell or lease fast. But with so many moving parts, closings take time and attention. You'll run into sellers who don't want to close for a month or two. Others are under serious pressure to close immediately. Regardless, it is crucial to allow yourself enough time to close, otherwise you risk your reputation, the opportunity, and any deposit you have made. This underlies the importance of having a good team to work with.

While some investor-buyers as well as lenders advertise being able to close in as little as three days, this is more a rarity than reality. For the cash investor, it is possible to close in three days, and it's also possible if you are using a private money lender with whom you have an established relationship and track record of success.

But when you are looking for institutional investment property funding through a hard money lender, the safer bet is a ten-day closing, which is entirely possible when you have your ducks in a row and come in well prepared. But often, it's the small things that can take time. And they can add up. That doesn't account for any hiccups either. Title and insurance can take a couple of days. Sometimes appraisers are backed up at least a couple of weeks. Then there may be holidays or nonbusiness days that can slow things down. What if your loan processor gets sick and has to pass your file to someone else?

For more traditional lending sources like a local bank, forty-five days is now seen as the standard and provides a more realistic and comfortable timeline.

Steps Involved in Closing a Real Estate Deal

After getting preapproved for financing and screening potential deals, getting to closing requires:

1. Making your offer and negotiating the contract
2. Making your formal loan application
3. Commissioning due diligence items (e.g., inspections, quotes, appraisals)
4. Obtaining insurances and any necessary approvals
5. Satisfying any underwriting conditions
6. Coordinating the closing
7. Finalizing the closing, title exchange, and funding

Things That Will Slow You Down

Crying Wolf: Rushing Your Vendors Unnecessarily

All of the steps listed previously are "sprints." And they must be given enough time to be completed. If every single one of your deals is an urgent "rush" for your vendors and partners, you risk burning them out and lose credibility. Allow them time to do their jobs well while still getting the job done. Build relationships, and try to reserve the big favors for when you really need them.

Busy Markets

Sometimes delays are simply a matter of the market being overwhelmed with volume. Appraisers, inspectors, and contractors can sometimes be backed up for weeks. These must-do items can hold back underwriting of loans. This doesn't mean to avoid these markets, but it is important to be alert to current turnaround times, making sure your contracts and closing dates accommodate them.

Inexperienced Partners and Vendors

What really slows down the loan process and closings more than anything is a vendor that fails to alert you to potential issues immediately. In a busy market, it may be because they are just busy themselves. In other cases, it's lack of experience. They don't recognize potential problems in advance. This is especially true when it comes to appraisals, titles, and contractors. Waiting until the day of closing to tell you that the seller's ex-spouse needs to be hunted down in another state to agree and sign the contract just isn't cool. You need professionals who know the business and lender's requirements and who will be proactive about keeping your deals moving.

Chain Transactions

Having multiple deals lined up is great. However, having multiple deals relying on each other to close can be risky. If you are waiting on one closing to fund the down payment on another property, there is a lot that can go wrong. The more links in the chain, the more likely there will be delays. Try to line up additional sources of capital and credit lines to ensure that you can close, even if there are delays.

When You Close—Watch the Calendar

Friday afternoon, the end of the month, and during any holiday can be tough times to close. They are just prone to issues. And delays can then run days or weeks longer versus a matter of hours. When you schedule your closing, be sure to ask the closer or scheduler about any upcoming calendar gotchas that could send your deal into a tailspin.

Three Roadblocks to Watch For

Roadblock 1: Watch the Lender Timelines

It is important for real estate investors to understand individual lenders' timelines. Know how long it takes to:

- Get through processing (the loan application and related documentation)
- Move through underwriting (the lender's assessment of the risk of writing the loan)
- Clear all of the conditions
- Receive a solid loan commitment
- Prepare the approved loans for closing

For example, once loan conditions are sent in, it may take at least forty-eight business hours to sign off on them (if they are accepted).

Then it can take another couple of days after final approval to get to close status. And then another three days to actually get to funding. Get to know your lender's processes so that you can be prepared for any detours.

Roadblock 2: Keep the Pressure On

While putting an extended closing date on your contract can theoretically give you more cushion, it can also leave others slacking. They are working on files in order of priority by closing. But you don't want your file collecting dust for a month before even being looked at. Make sure to keep the pressure on and ensure that consistent progress is being made. In addition, the introduction of new Truth in Lending Act disclosure rules in 2015 changed the way lenders and closing attorneys process and fund loans. Be sure your team is well aware of guidelines and processes so that you're not caught unaware.

Roadblock 3: It's Not Closed Until It's Funded (and Then Some)

"Don't count your chickens until they've hatched." Don't count on the money until it is not just closed, but you've got the money in your hand. And note that in fraudulent deals, money can still get yanked back.

Preparing for Closing Day

Ensuring smooth sailing through the closing requires being prepared for the closing. That means making sure your ID is valid, you have the cash available to close, and all parties are free to sign.

Savvy investors recognize that actually converting an acquisition into profit also requires renting or reselling. The faster that is arranged, the faster returns actually happen. So make sure property management, renovation teams, and the marketing team and collateral are all ready to go on the day of closing.

Be sure you have a system for keeping documents stored and ready. And after closing, don't forget the thank-you cards and gifts for those you've built relationships with.

Going even further, document your takeaways from each transaction. What went well? What could have been done better? Many seasoned investors whom I've talked to say they wish they had kept "what happened" notes to help them learn from past closings to improve future ones as well.

TAKEAWAYS

- *What are the key actions you can take to ensure a smooth and timely closing?*

30

AVOIDING COSTLY
BORROWING MISTAKES

Understanding the Underlying Costs of Funding

When it comes to accurately estimating your real estate deal costs, you've got to avoid omitting costs that you may not have considered. Optimizing per-deal, annual, and lifetime profit from real estate is just as much about avoiding costly transactional blunders as it is making the big bucks. So, what should investors pay specific attention to if they want to minimize losses and waste?

Earnest Money Deposits

Deposits represent one of the biggest risks to investors, and one of the most common ways to lose money. There are three parts to protecting your deposit money. You need to protect:

1. Where your deposit money is held
2. The strength of your purchase contract
3. How effectively investors live up to contract terms

Deposit Smarts

Obviously the smaller the deposit a buyer makes on an offer to purchase, the lower the financial risk. Of course, sellers know this, and they and their agents will try to secure the biggest deposit possible. The hotter the market, the more negotiating power the selling side has, which ultimately impacts the required deposit to lock down a deal. Decide in advance of negotiations how much you are willing to risk for this deal and opportunity. Avoid "auction fever" when bidding on properties that have multiple offers and require highest and best offers with high deposit requirements.

Who Holds the Deposit Money?

The designated holder of an earnest money deposit is one of the most pivotal parts of this risk equation. It is the seller and selling agent's intention to get the deposit money locked down. At a minimum they'll request that it is deposited in their real estate broker's escrow account. Investors must be aware that this is the equivalent of saying goodbye to the money in the event the contract falls apart.

When things go well, the money will be credited at closing. If the contract falls apart, often it isn't easy to get back. By simply disputing the escrowed money, a seller and agent can effectively tie up your cash. In some cases, you can burn more in time and legal fees than you would have lost by letting earnest money go. In these cases, you've got to know when to stop throwing time and money away.

To avoid this happening, whenever possible all earnest money deposits should be made with your own real estate attorney or trusted title company. This ensures that the money is being managed by someone on your side.

Real Estate Contract Contingencies

A well-written real estate purchase contract provides great protection for your earnest money deposit. This is the document that provides the contingencies under which you can back out of the contract and are eligible to get your deposit back.

Expect sellers and their agents to push back on contingencies in order to tie you in, because they want a guarantee they'll at least walk with your deposit money. Be wise. Give yourself outs and give yourself plenty of time for due diligence.

Common contingencies that savvy investors use to protect themselves include appraisal contingencies, financing contingencies, and inspection contingencies. Then if you, as the buyer, can't get the financing you hoped for, property inspections uncover bigger issues than you budgeted for, or the property doesn't appraise for as much as you thought, you can choose to walk away and get your deposit back—or renegotiate.

Note that most of these items are extremely time-sensitive. You must be sure that you can get an inspector and appraiser out to the property, and get financing within the allotted time, or you could lose the deal and your money. Check on vendors' current timelines before inking the contract.

Due Diligence Costs

Due diligence is critical. However, it can also burn a lot of working capital. Given the risks to deposits, and the stubbornness of some sellers and real estate agents to grant terms, some due diligence can be done up front. Other due diligence is done only after a contract is signed without the investor having the real, hard numbers on the deal.

If you end up spending money on multiple inspections or environmental reports and multiple appraisals and title searches—all before closing on one deal—that equals net profits that effectively come out of that one deal.

Savvy investors know their local markets intimately and do as much preliminary due diligence as they can for free online, and by calling their preferred vendors, before getting locked in.

Buying Property Sight Unseen

Investing in an out of area property without physically walking it first is commonplace in busy real estate times. This is true of auction properties, third-party deals out of state, and even local deals when in a hurry. Sometimes these deals turn out to be incredibly profitable. But it is a big risk. There are many factors that can impact value and costs. Make no assumptions. For example, photos can miss that the wiring or connections for major appliances are outdated. Find that out after closing and you're looking at thousands of dollars in contractor work to rewire the property. What if a single street view was missed and it is a commercial building? Many lenders won't make residential loans on properties that may be considered to be in commercial areas.

To make a safe out-of-area investment, it pays to use a broker's price opinion (BPO) service that, for a fee, sends a professional to the subject property to give a valuation and property report. Sometimes a BPO alone is not enough and investors are well served to hire a local inspector to give the property a once-over—in fact, it may even be a lender requirement—to ensure that due diligence was performed on the property and that project and property planning are well executed.

Sabotaging Your Loan Application

There are a number of very expensive mistakes that investors can make that have the potential to derail their loan applications, or that result in inferior terms when it comes to closing time.
These items include:

- Applying for any other credit during the loan approval process
- Having too many lenders check your credit
- Increasing debt balances and payments

- Quitting a job
- Failing to maintain a paper trail of money being moved around
- Skipping payments
- Executing new deals that impact your loan currently in consideration

It is traditional that lenders and other parties will perform last-minute checks on the day of closing to verify that all of the loan information is still accurate. This includes employment, the status of corporate entities, income, and credit scores, for example.

Title and Lien Searches

Title and lien searches should be updated the day of closing. It is crucial that no new potential liens are levied against the property that could add to your debt, affect the ability to resell, or impact your ownership rights. A good title company should have you covered here. You might not always like what they find, but it is in your best interest. For this reason, among many others, it is absolutely vital that investors find a reputable and trustworthy title company or closing attorney committed to doing business right. It is better to pay a little more for a good title partner than risk the costs of working with a "get what you pay for" provider.

In the downturn of the early 2000s, some title companies failed to pay off mortgages and didn't pay property taxes for which they collected escrow money. Some were even raided by the FBI—wreaking havoc with all of their clients' files and properties. Get a reputable title agent on your side.

Accurately Forecasting Closing Time Frames

Missing closing dates is consistently one of the most expensive challenges for real estate investors. If you don't close on schedule, your earnest money deposit is effectively forfeited to the seller. Loan rate locks could expire, interest rates could go up, and other issues will arise. Don't miss your closing date. It has a snowball effect, and when you are in the midst of a closing, it pays to check and double-check that all the moving parts are doing exactly that—moving toward the closing.

Give your deal plenty of time to close. Know how long it is taking your lender to close on your type of transaction, and add some time padding to that. Hard money loans may close very quickly. But conventional residential home loans and commercial real estate loans can take a lot longer. This can also vary depending on the market and season in which you are trying to close.

Since the TILA-RESPA Integrated Disclosure (TRID) rules were implemented in October 2015, the National Association of Realtors (NAR) has recommended allowing at least forty-five days from contract to close, versus the previous standard of thirty days. TILA refers to the Truth in Lending Act and RESPA the Real Estate Settlement Procedures Act. The head of the Mortgage Bankers Association cites the new TRID rules as one of the biggest changes to disrupt the industry that affects every single lender, real estate agent, investor, and consumer involved.

The most notable element of the new TRID rules is a three-day waiting period between the final terms being presented and actual completion of the transaction. There is a danger that some people will encounter a vicious cycle where this three-day period resets several times, causing far more extensive delays. Watch out for it and, as always, be prepared.

Failure to Hit the Ground Running

Every day that an investor holds a property it means money. Most significantly, it means holding costs. The day you get the keys, your contractor team should be on the job and marketing for tenants, or resale should be in the works.

There are plenty of expenses involved in buying real estate. There is also plenty investors can do to minimize costs and avoid losses. Use this chapter as a checklist to slash waste and maximize profit potential. Make sure you have a great attorney on retainer. Commit to operating efficiently.

TAKEAWAYS

- *What are the key actions you can take to ensure a smooth and timely closing?*

31

INVESTMENT PROPERTY LOANS

Everything Is Negotiable, Right?

The Toll Booth—How Much Will It Cost to Get Your Deal Funded?

Financial leverage is the ultimate power tool for real estate investors, but there are costs of borrowing. How much does it cost to get funded? How can investors reduce those costs of doing business?

The Power of Leverage

We are all well aware of the dangers of over-leverage or borrowing from notorious Hollywood-style loan sharks. Yet there is no denying that financial leverage is a critical part of real estate investing, personal income, and wealth building.

The advantages of leverage include:

- Being able to invest in better quality properties and deals
- Investing for higher returns
- Enabling diversification

- Reducing risk
- Propelling gains and goals

The investor who leverages an additional $1 million in real estate today, and who is able to achieve just an average net return of 7.5 percent over the next ten years, would pocket an extra $1,061,031.56, thanks to compounding returns. Not too shabby, right?

Those results can always be scaled in volume, and time, too. You can use online compound interest calculators like Moneychimp to play with the numbers yourself.

Borrowing Costs + Investment Strategy

Borrowing the money to leverage real estate costs money. That's how lenders make their money so that they can stay around and help you on future deals. The truly wealthy and savvy investors actually want their vendors, partners, and lenders to be fairly compensated. They understand the value in paying their vendors and partners a fair share.

However, the wealthy and successful are also known for being prudent with their financial choices. That means not unnecessarily overpaying. As financial icon Warren Buffett famously put it in the simplest terms, "Don't lose money." Let's look at some of the borrowing costs that you can (and should) negotiate and save on. What's most important before negotiating and shopping around for capital is to understand your goals and what type of borrowing strategy best aligns with your real estate investment strategy and goals.

There are four ways to strategize your funding costs:

1. Weighing higher up front costs with lower costs later
2. Postponing costs until later
3. Prioritizing lower payments and cash flow versus cost
4. Focusing on reducing total net borrowing costs

The approach you choose depends on your resources and the types of deals you are doing. For example, hard money may appear more expensive, but if it allows investors to gain better deals it may not mean a significant hit. Remember, part of something is better than all of nothing. Rental property investors may seek lower rates to maximize cash flow. Others just need to maximize financing up front so that they can generate larger sums later.

Common Borrowing Costs and Fees

Common costs associated with investment property loans include:

- Interest payments
- Prepayment penalties (in some states)
- Mortgage insurance
- Title insurance
- Property insurance
- Origination fees
- Points
- Application fees
- Underwriting fees
- Credit report fees
- Recording fees
- Transfer and sales taxes
- Prorated property taxes up front

Some of these costs are directly related to the loan and are lender fees. Others are third-party fees such as title and insurance costs. Others are local government fees (i.e., taxes and recording fees).

Everything Is Negotiable, Right?

Yes and no. Some costs, like government taxes, are hard costs. While you can't negotiate the government fees, you can negotiate for your seller or buyer to pay them. Fees like lender points are more flexible. Everything is negotiable in terms of who pays what, and how much. So yes, everything is negotiated in some sense. However, your lender and other vendors will certainly have minimums they need to meet.

In most cases it is pretty easy to get lenders to shift costs around to meet your needs. This is how "no closing cost" loans are possible. It doesn't mean they are free. It just means that they may absorb some of the up-front charges by rolling them into the loan and charging more interest. Those who want to pay less each month may choose to pay more points to reduce interest and monthly payments.

Use your loan estimate from your lender to shop and compare loan quotes with other lenders. Note that the annual percentage rate (APR) figure is usually the most significant in accurately comparing loan quotes and the true total cost of borrowing. Yet, you can't afford not to make sure prepayment penalties, terms, and other factors are equal as well.

Negotiating Smarts

It never hurts to ask your loan officer to "do a little better" or drop a certain fee. Often that's all it takes. However, investors must also know when to stop. If you've got a great loan officer, good lender, and a good loan offer that you can make work—go with the flow!

Prospective borrowers can absolutely go too far in negotiating. There is definitely a point at which the lender will no longer deem it worthwhile to win your business or close your loan. Beyond the risk of lending to you, the lender knows there are other borrowers out there who may be willing to pay more for the money and with less hassle. It takes a lot of people a lot of hours to work to get your loan funded. Would you flip houses or rent properties out for free? No one can afford to keep doing that.

It is also critical to note that in most cases speed, closing on time, and just actually getting your loan closed are probably worth more than spending extra hours trying to shave another $100 off an already great loan offer. So, try to get slightly reduced lender fees, and work with title and insurance companies to knock off a few bucks where you can, too. But know when you've got a good deal that you don't want to blow.

Quick Tips for Negotiating Better Loan Deals

1. Talk to your loan officer about your goals and needs, and find out how they can arrange the terms to best suit you.
2. Make sure you are comparing quotes in an apples-to-apples way.
3. Always ask, "Can you do any better?"
4. Know when to take a good deal.

TAKEAWAYS

- *Prepare to fund your next property. Make a list of common lender fees. Then, do some preliminary research to get estimated costs for each type of fee. Use this same list as a checklist when you are comparing loan costs.*

32

HOW TO CHOOSE THE BEST FUNDING AND INVESTMENT PROPERTY LENDER TO MEET YOUR NEEDS

Taking Different Paths to Reach the Same Destination

Despite what most people think, there are a lot of investment property lenders out there. Billions of dollars have poured into private and hard money—and that capital is readily available for the average investor to fund projects of all kinds. So how do real estate investors choose the best ones to work with? Why not just settle in and work with one lender?

All lenders offer financial leverage that may be used to take you to your goals. And building relationships with mortgage lenders and capital sources is important, but there are many choices, and sometimes it is not only wise but necessary to shake things up. When is it time to bond with a lender? Break up with one? Mix it up?

Picking the Right Lender for Your Project

Investors often find themselves switching their game plan due to personal goals or market changes. Or they adopt new strategies as they progress over the course of their investment lifetime. Get to know the right funding for your investment type and shop the best lenders to meet your particular needs.

For a number of reasons it is often unrealistic to use the same lender for every deal that you'll ever do. You may use the same loan broker or lending portal, but the individual financiers will almost certainly differ over time and between transactions.

Five Scenarios That Demand Multiple Lenders

1. Really big deals
2. When switching between strategies with the same property
3. When engaging in different real estate investment strategies
4. When investing in different geographic locations
5. When reaching a lender's limits

Different Types of Lending Sources

- Conventional banks
- Credit unions
- Crowdfunding
- Hard money lenders
- Private mortgage lenders
- Land loan specialists

It's not uncommon for bigger deals to require a variety of funding, including the investor's own cash combined with commercial lender loans or even crowdfunding. In the case of a fix and hold, a hard money loan may be used to acquire the property and obtain rehab funds. After work is complete and the property is rented, the property may be refinanced on more attractive terms on a long-term loan.

Regardless of strategy, geography, experience, and other factors, many lenders have restrictions on loans they will underwrite for a single borrower, including the number of loans or a dollar amount, in order to limit their exposure to loss.

The Importance of Investor-Lender Relationships

Even though it pays to work with multiple lenders, relationships are important. Relationships with lenders, loan officers, and other vendors can make all the difference in getting more and better real estate deals done, improving your investment performance, and gaining a competitive advantage in the marketplace.

Once you have some deal volume, investors are often flooded with offers of credit. You'll even have competing lenders and title reps stopping by to take you to lunch or happy hour—all in an effort to win your business. Remember, they need investors as much as investors need them. But until then, it's on you as the investor to do a lot of the relationship building.

Making the effort to build relationships has a great payoff. You know what they say: "Your network is your net worth," and your network can carry a ton of weight when it comes to getting better terms and loan deals, getting rushed files closed on time, and shuffling closing fees to make the numbers work at closing.

The Reality of the Lender Relationship

You may develop friendships with your loan officers, title reps, home inspectors, and other industry professionals. But when it comes to lending entities, you shouldn't count on a "one and only," long-term relationship. Why? Especially when you've developed such great working relationships? It is important to know that every lender goes through phases and cycles. What may be a great lender to work with this year may not be next year. Lenders may run into financial challenges or changes in underwriting guidelines; they may take heavy losses on one type of property or loan profile or, over time, they may find regulations in your state or zip code unattractive to deal with.

Over time your borrowing needs will change, too. You may move into multifamily deals, commercial property investing, or another asset class—and that means you may need a new lender who specializes in that particular investment type.

Another reason you can't count on long-term relationships is that an investment property lender will often sell loans after they are processed and closed. Most often you'll deal with someone completely different when it comes to loan servicing next year.

Giving a lot of business volume to the same vendors and lenders over time can give you some pull in some cases, but don't expect that loyalty to be reciprocated as much as you think—especially when working with the larger financing companies. Ten years and $10 million is barely a blip for a multibillion-dollar lender that has been around for decades.

Investment Property Lenders Need You Too

Too often, investors have a one-sided view of the lender-borrower relationship. Never forget: Lenders need you too. Loan officers need you too. New loans are their commission, profit, and paychecks. If your project is a winner and you are a good risk and can help them deploy capital and boost originations, they will aggressively seek your business. They spend millions of dollars on trying to get the attention of investors in an effort to attract and keep borrowers. Consistent repeat business saves them massive amounts of money and increases their operating profit. But remember, every lender isn't always a good fit. When terms and relationships aren't working, don't try to force it. There's another investment property lender out there that offers the type of capital you need.

TAKEAWAYS

- *Think about the types of properties and projects you plan to invest in.*
- *Next, make a list of each property type. Identify the different types of lenders you can utilize and begin researching available funding sources for each.*

33

HIGH-PERFORMANCE PROPERTY FINANCING

Understanding the Mechanics of Your Loan

How to Keep Your Loans Rolling Through till Closing

Investors looking for an uneventful trip during closing after closing need to master how the loan process works, how to best manage their lenders, and how to sail through at the closing table.

Just How Much Does It Matter?

Understanding the loan process and knowing how to effectively manage a real estate transaction makes all the difference in successful and profitable closings. To get through to closing and get your deals done requires knowing how lenders work. Plus, you have to anticipate issues and know how to motivate the different players to work to your benefit. Without this skill set, it certainly means deals are at risk for falling apart. Or at best, you'll have costly delays or get stuck with inferior terms and less profit. And any one of those can mean the difference between a good deal and a dud.

Great investors get to know their lenders' processes and under-writing guidelines nearly as well as their lenders, underwriters, and loan officers—and they are able to get deals done, and on terms others can't.

How the Loan Process Works

Most borrowers would be floored if they understood a fraction of what goes on behind the scenes at the typical closing. In fact, given the complexity and the number of people and factors involved, it's a sheer miracle that any loans get closed at all. Signing the contract and making the loan application is just the very beginning and is only a minute part of the process.

While each lender and loan type is different, the loan process generally flows like this:

1. Official loan application and paperwork documentation are submitted.
2. Loan goes into processing.
3. Due diligence and third-party items are ordered (e.g., credit, appraisals).
4. Loan goes to underwriting.
5. Conditional loan approval is granted.
6. Loan conditions are received, reviewed, and approved.
7. Loan moves to closing department.
8. Closing documents are drawn and a Closing Disclosure is sent out.
9. Closing is scheduled.
10. Closing documents are signed and reviewed so that funding can be approved.

This is the dramatically scaled-down version of the process for most institutional mortgage loans. In some cases, asset-based loans can be much easier, with fewer steps and individuals involved.

Managing Your Loan

Managing your loan and loan process is something that isn't even on the radar of most new investors. They expect it to take care of itself. It doesn't. It is a process that needs daily attention.

One of three people must take ownership of managing the transaction:

1. You
2. Your loan officer
3. Your real estate agent (when applicable)

Managing the loan should be left to these professionals only if they have mastered this process and can manage and coordinate everyone else involved. A mortgage broker is usually the most efficient at this process. Realtors and mortgage professionals can deliver their best value here, too. But if you don't have power people in these positions and you are doing serious volume, then you may want to have a member of your own team monitor the loan process.

Managing the loan process means:

- Organizing and preparing paperwork and documents
- Coordinating inspections and third-party items
- Doing consistent follow-up
- Coordinating the closing, and ensuring that all parties are adequately prepared to close

Tip: Don't overdo it and micromanage everyone. Push for results, but do it in a way that gets people to hustle for you without being a pest. Calling and emailing people too frequently is counterproductive and slows down the process. Establish the best methods of contact in advance and set timelines with your lender to receive updates and clear conditions.

What to Expect at the Closing Table

Getting to the closing can sometimes be a marathon of Indy 500 proportions. It can be a huge relief when you finally cross the finish line. But there can also be glitches.

Today's closings differ significantly from closings in the past. A few decades ago everyone met up at the title company or real estate attorney's office. Both realtors would be there. The loan officer or mortgage broker would be there. Both buyer and seller would be present. And a title company closing rep, or at least one attorney, would be there to walk the parties through the paperwork, guide signatures, and notarize them.

Today, this would definitely be the exception rather than the rule. More likely today you will run to the closing office and sign your half of the paperwork with the closer, or they'll come out to your home or office. Or if you are really fortunate you can do the whole thing online.

New rules dictate that the Closing Disclosure (which used to be the HUD-1 Settlement Statement) must be provided to all parties three days before actual consummation of the transaction. It used to be twenty-four hours, but all too often the parties would show up at the closing to find the final terms far different from expected. The pressure they were under in that moment led to most simply signing whatever was in front of them. And some unscrupulous individuals counted on that. The newer rule's intent is to eliminate closing table disputes. Everyone should now have the opportunity to dispute errors and get them fixed. But it is also important to note that under the TRID rules, this can cause that three-day period to reset all over again—which is another reason that the closing process needs careful daily attention.

Being Prepared to Close: A Checklist

* Have an original, valid government-issued ID with at least several months before expiry.

- Have more than enough liquid cash to close and available for wire (most closing offices no longer accept a cashier's check but instead require funds to be wired directly to the closing account).
- Have any additional documents to be required at closing (e.g., proof of debts paid off, proof of work done to the property).

Post-Closing Considerations

Make sure you are ready to navigate any roadblocks that can arise after closing. It's also helpful to make notes that will help you prepare for the next real estate closing.

- Maintain a contact list of everyone involved in the transaction.
- Jot down any unusual aspects of the closing that can be helpful for future closings.
- Keep records of all paperwork and files.
- Be sure to document any changes to the property, and know where to find the information.
- Have multiple backups of this data, online and offline.

Do not underestimate the power and importance of understanding how the loan process works and how to effectively manage transactions, and stay equipped with protected data to facilitate smooth future closings. Many deals have been lost due to a messy closing. Be proactive and be prepared.

TAKEAWAYS

- *As you begin funding your next deal, make a list of questions for your lender and closing agent. If you are using a realtor, start there to get answers. If you are handling the purchase yourself, get answers from your lender and closer.*

34

FIX AND FLIP STRATEGIES TO GET YOUR INVESTMENT PROPERTY SOLD

What Smart Tactics Can Help Real Estate Investors Go from Flip to Flip with Ease?

The profit from flipping just one property can be substantial. And some deals even eclipse the typical average annual earnings of other investments, making it a very attractive way to make a living. Most investors want to keep the machine turning properties quarter after quarter or even month after month. Getting from deal number one to flipping investment properties every month, or even dozens of properties every month, requires effective processes. How do you efficiently turn that first acquisition into a house-flipping cash snowball?

Tips for Fixing and Flipping Fast

Each real estate investment opportunity is only as good as the execution. For flippers, potential profit only becomes a reality when the rehab work is done, the property is resold, and the cash is firmly in hand. So, to convert opportunities efficiently and consistently, what are some of the smart rules that successful property flippers stick to?

Renovate to Your Target Market to Sell Fast

Would you put granite counters and stainless steel appliances in a cookie-cutter starter home? Gut instinct says no. But even as obvious as it seems, there are exceptions. For example, a cookie-cutter starter home in San Diego may command relatively low-cost upgrades, but the same style and size home in Boise couldn't get you the same kind of return. Be smart with your renovation choices. Carefully consider who your buyer is: What are the buyer's hot buttons and what are the must-haves that you can offer without breaking your rehab budget? With experience, you'll know how to identify your target buyers and make even smarter rehab choices.

Here's how you unlock profit with better processes:

1. Hit the ground running with boots on the job from day one. You should start your renovation plans long before closing.
2. Build strong relationships by managing and paying contractors well. A good team of contractors is critical to repeat flipping.
3. Don't waste materials and tools because they'll always come in handy later. Serial flippers have readily available tools and inventory to get the job done.
4. Commit to quality rehab work to preserve and build your reputation. That's how you get buyers under contract before the project is even completed.
5. Be sure to include a marketing budget in your initial figures. In fact, check your numbers and check them again to make sure your project is on track financially.
6. Recognize the critical role that marketing plays in profit and resales.

When to Start Marketing for Resale

When is the right time to begin marketing to resell your flips? This can be the most contentious phase of the house-flipping process. Even the experts are often split on when to start marketing properties for sale.

Realtors are decidedly in favor of only beginning active advertising and showings after the property is 100 percent polished, cleaned, and often even staged. Of course, this works in the agent's favor as it theoretically makes it a lot easier to sell at top dollar. That means more profit and commission for real estate agents.

However, every day means more holding costs that bleed money and profit. Some savvy rehabbers choose to begin marketing the opportunity from day one of the acquisition. Some may even market before that. The less you have to put in, and the less time it takes to resell, the lower the risk and the higher the profit potential. In many cases this may also be the ideal scenario for the buyer, because some buyers would rather complete improvements to their own tastes.

The downside of beginning to market too early is that some buyers may not have the imagination to envision the end product and value and are scared away from an unfinished project. It depends on the buyer and how you are able to present the property. If you can afford it, test out these options.

Choosing the Right Real Estate Marketing Formula for Your Deals

There's more than one way to market an investment property for sale. Choosing the right path can depend on:

- Your location
- Your overall real estate investment strategy and business model

- Your funding arrangements and loan terms
- The specific property characteristics
- Current and trending market conditions
- Your deal numbers
- The ideal target buyers for this property

Reselling the Property

What, then, are some of the common ways to resell a property? How do they stack up compared to your needs and goals?

Listing Property with a Real Estate Agent

The right real estate agent can be an effective marketing partner. Several notable house-flipping personalities from reality shows like *Flip This House* use realtors to market and sell their properties. Other long-time investors have launched their own real estate brokerages to sell their properties. Even Warren Buffett jumped into the brokerage scene with Berkshire Hathaway Home Services. For the average investor, working with a local, knowledgeable agent can be a plus.

There are some downsides to listing properties with a realtor. Commission is a big one. You'll have to decide for yourself what an agent's service is worth. Plus, there will always be those who will negotiate fees. But perhaps even more significant is the time factor. If agents are trying to lock you up with a six- or twelve-month listing agreement, with no guarantee it will sell during that period, most flippers can't afford that. Savvy flippers are trying to be in and out of deals in ninety days or less. Another factor is how long you have on your loan term. If you only have a six-month asset-based loan, you absolutely have no business in signing a twelve-month listing agreement.

There are upsides to working with agents, such as access to the multiple listing service (MLS) and a wider audience, and having a professional out there working for you. Just make sure you do the math carefully.

Some real estate investors choose to obtain their own real estate licenses. Again, carefully do the math on the costs and time demands. And watch for legal restrictions on your investment activities.

Hybrid Real Estate Services

There are hybrid services that can offer many of the same benefits of listing with a realtor, without the cost. These can generally be divided into two categories:

1. Flat-fee listing services offered by licensed real estate brokerages
2. For-sale-by-owner (FSBO) services

With around 60 percent of home sales happening via the MLS, the first option shouldn't be dismissed. If you can list your property on the MLS for a couple hundred dollars, that may be smart usage of part of your real estate marketing budget. You'll represent yourself as the seller and a buyer's agent will bring the buyer. You'll still have to offer commission to the buyer's agent, but in most cases it's half the cost of the typical MLS listing—because there is no seller's agent commission. Before choosing this option, ask yourself if you realistically have the time and expertise to sell on your own.

FSBO services are also available. For-sale-by-owner websites and publications can offer another marketing avenue. When selling properties on your own without the services of a real estate agent, be sure you understand your contracts, deadlines, and commitments.

DIY Marketing

There are many ways that real estate investors can market their own properties for sale themselves. They include:

- Yard signs
- "Bandit" signs
- Newspaper and magazine ads

- Email marketing
- Social media marketing
- Pay-per-click and other online marketing

All of these marketing methods work. They can all also run on their own cycles, becoming more or less effective during certain phases. In a strong seller's market, sometimes all it takes is a yard sign or a Craigslist ad to sell a property in a few hours. In tough times it can take a lot more money and a lot more time.

The Buyers List

Serious real estate investors, who are eager to build robust deal flow and maximize profit while limiting risk, make building a buyers list a priority—especially when wholesaling properties. Put simply, if you have a list of qualified buyers eagerly waiting to purchase properties from you, investors can quickly and easily flip houses like clockwork.

As you are marketing your renovated properties, add as many qualified buyers to your list as possible. This can be done through premarketing the home to contacts made through your online marketing, such as Craigslist and social media, along with bandit sign and direct-mail campaigns.

The process of turning a property into profits is one that, when mastered, can generate a lot of income. Every investor takes a slightly different route to profits; the most successful investors have funding, a team, and a set of general "get it done" processes to take a project to completion.

🏘 TAKEAWAYS

The growth of your real estate investing depends on how you can scale your business. Flippers doing only one or two properties each year may not be concerned with scale. But those who want to grow must scale out.

- *What is your target annual flipping income? How many houses would you need to flip to get there? If it's more than two, can you scale your business for multiple annual flips?*
- *Map out a plan.*

35

BUY AND HOLD
REAL ESTATE INVESTMENT

Maximizing Income Property Opportunities

Some investors make acquisitions with the expressed goal of turning them into buy and hold income properties. Others make the decision after they make the purchase and the numbers or market justify holding versus flipping. A few others may feel they have little choice after renovating or flipping plans are disrupted.

So when is it time to hold?

When the numbers make sense.

Strategic buy and hold real estate investors always "make their money when they buy." That can mean positive cash flow from rental income or buying with a significant equity cushion. Stay far away from negative cash flow, or overpaying and solely gambling on appreciation for profit. Buy and hold properties must support themselves from the income they can generate. Gambling in the real estate market has bankrupted millions of people. It is not a gamble when you acquire undervalued assets with built-in equity.

 Thinking about holding onto a property for a while? How can you improve the numbers? What critical factors do you need to consider and ultimately master to make "buy and hold" real estate profitable?

There are three factors most investors will want to check when deciding if it is time to hold:

1. Real net operating income (NOI)—discussed in more detail in Chapter 22
2. Potential for consistent, long-term cash flow
3. Potential for positive appreciation

What if the numbers don't work?

Refinancing and Optimizing Financial Leverage

After the rehab work is done, there should be even more equity in the property. Once rented, you also have rental income to help qualify for a new loan. If the property was financed with shorter-term hard or private money, this is a great time to refinance to lock in lower rate, and lower payment, long-term financing.

 Sometimes the current numbers just won't work for buying and holding a property. Perhaps you used higher rate, asset-based lending because the condition of the property couldn't qualify for other loans. Or maybe it was because of the need for speed. Perhaps the payments can't be supported by the property and its rental income. Maybe there's a balloon payment in the next thirty-six months. What do you do?

For example, refinancing a $250,000 loan with a 7 percent interest rate and thirty-year amortization payments to a 4 percent interest rate would drop your debt service from $1,663.26 per month to just $1,193.54. That's a substantial extra spread for creating real positive cash flow each month.

Another option is taking out a line of credit. This could be used to pay off any existing debt, provide access to additional capital for making future acquisitions, and serve as a security cushion for unexpected expenses and maintenance. Credit can also help avoid leaving equity captive in your properties when it should be working hard to help you achieve your financial goals.

For some scenarios, lenders may even offer mini-perms, or "one-time close" construction-to-permanent loans. These loans automatically roll over into more attractive loans after the rehab work is done or a property proves its income potential. The big benefit: It's all done with one closing and one set of closing costs. Lenders offer these types of loans because they are based on the value of the property after it's been improved and increased in value.

What's the Best Leasing Strategy?

The numbers can also be improved by finding the optimal leasing strategy for your property.

There is certainly more than one option, including:

1. Annual and long-term leases
2. Seasonal vacation rentals
3. Airbnb-style short-term rentals
4. Extended stay rentals (i.e., not weekly, but not annual)
5. Corporate rentals

The last four of these options can offer substantially higher monthly rents than your neighbors are getting on annual leases. While there can be cons as well as pros for these strategies, they are worth exploring in order to maximize income. There are more turnovers, but the cost can be covered by the increased rental rate.

Intelligent Tenant Screening

Ensuring consistent cash flow and maximizing NOI relies on the landlord's tenant screening and selection process. Rental turnovers are costly. Thorough screening can keep turnovers at a minimum.

Tenant screening and selection is very important; in fact, it can be make-or-break for the landlord. But it is even more important for real estate investors to find balance in this process. The key is understanding your local rental market conditions, available tenant pool, and the high cost of vacancies.

Many newbie landlords get hung up on an extreme vetting process or they don't do it at all. Both are counterproductive. In certain top-end markets, investors may be able to demand top-notch credit scores and substantial deposits. In other markets, they may not be able to find tenants with 600+ credit scores, or who are willing to pay application fees. In some cases it may be a struggle to collect several months' security deposit up front or to demand clean background checks, even if they are legal in your area. At the other extreme, you find landlords who don't ask enough questions or do enough screening, and the results can be disastrous.

Vacancies cost money every day. Vacant properties can bring extra risk to the asset too, such as vandalism and squatters. If you are not getting applicants or filing the property on the terms you are requesting, back up and regroup—adjust your marketing and terms.

Property Maintenance and Management

Property maintenance and daily management often has the most significant impact on real net profit or loss when it comes to income real estate. The biggest choice here is whether to take the DIY approach and self-manage, or to outsource and hire a professional third-party property management firm.

In many cases, outsourcing this part of the business makes sense. Using a third-party property management firm frees up investors to keep sourcing new acquisitions and focus on building their business. If you decide to self-manage, be sure to leave room in your cash flow for hiring a manager, as one day you may not want or be able to manage it anymore.

Buy and hold real estate investments make sense for a lot of investors. When house flipping no longer has appeal, building a portfolio of cash-flowing properties is a great way to go. There's passive income, tax advantages, and the potential for appreciation.

TAKEAWAYS

- *Do you see buy and hold investing in your future? If so, how can you transition from house flipping to buy and hold? What do you need to make it happen?*
- *Start mapping out a plan for the short and the long term. This will help you recognize and capitalize on opportunities as they arise.*

36

KEEP FUELING THE JOURNEY

How do property investors keep the wheels turning to go from deal to deal?

Once investors have the hang of funding and turning real estate opportunities into profitable ventures, how do they keep the wheels greased so that they can repeat and scale for even better results?

Lap After Lap

Achieving all your financial goals isn't likely to happen with just one real estate deal. It's a journey. It's a long-term venture. Even when individuals can afford to comfortably retire on their real estate profits, they need to keep their money safe and working hard for them. So after you fix and flip that first deal, or you successfully convert a property to a performing rental, how do you most efficiently keep the machine going to repeat win after win?

In Formula One racing, there are multiple laps and even multiple races. The key to success is not only getting into a good pattern for each following lap, but also making timely but brief pit stops between races to recalibrate engines and replace tires.

Performance-Boosting Analysis

In any sport, all serious participants take time to improve their performance. This time might be spent watching footage of the competition, training, getting better equipment, and doing maintenance.

In real estate, investors can boost performance by:

- Committing to constant learning
- Completing regular deal and portfolio analysis
- Targeting areas for improvement
- Diversifying
- Networking

After your first few real estate deals, and at least quarterly or annually after that, investors need to take time to evaluate their performance.

Specifically, make a list of what went well and what could be improved upon. Turn the things you did successfully and great into systems to be repeated and scaled. Target the areas that can be improved on for further development.

- Could you have done a little better in due diligence and estimating repair costs?
- How about negotiating slightly better loan terms, or managing the transaction through to closing?
- What went right and wrong with your rehab projects?
- How did your marketing go?

Quick Tips for Tuning Your Engine

- Systematize the process wherever possible.
- Keep great records.

- Look for tax saving strategies.
- Ask lenders about lines of credit and blanket mortgages for streamlined access to capital.

The Reality of Deal Flow

Stopping or slowing down because you think you've already won, only to be passed by a rival, is one of the most classic and cringeworthy bloopers. It may be painfully hilarious to watch it happen to others on YouTube, but when it comes to your income and wealth, it can be gut wrenching and leave a big and very real hole in your wallet.

Real estate transactions can have a significant fallout rate. It varies over time and depends a lot on how easy lending is, but it cannot be underestimated.

Serious and savvy investors may expect to investigate ten potential properties before making five offers, securing two contracts, and hoping at least one closes. Your numbers may be better or worse. Know them, and how many deals you need to look at each month, week, or day. Know how many offers you need to make—and how many contracts you need signed to meet your goals.

When investors merely make the occasional offer and stop looking once they find one of interest, they'll find that they go quite a while between actual closings. That isn't going to do wonders for steady progress toward goals or consistency of income, not to mention missing out on many profitable opportunities.

Tips for Improving Deal Flow

Multiple Sources

You know you need to find and do more deals, but how do you achieve that?

Consistency and volume are going to depend on having a variety of deal sources working all the time. The goal should be to have new deals to review in your inbox every day.

Here are eleven sources to put to work:

1. Property and funding sources like ConnectedInvestors.com and CiX.com
2. The multiple listing service (MLS) in your target investment area
3. Realtors
4. Craigslist and online sources
5. Real estate investment groups
6. Real estate wholesalers and bird dogs
7. Local contractors and vendors
8. Professional referral sources (e.g., loan officers, bank managers, attorneys)
9. Local newspapers
10. Your own website and lead-generating marketing
11. Driving through neighborhoods

Relationships

Getting great deals on properties that "may" be for sale is about finding properties that the rest of the world doesn't know about. If you want truly profitable deals and the chance to buy them at the best prices, on the best terms, then you want the first look before the general public. For example, real estate agents can bring you their pocket listings before anyone else. You may need to earn this privilege by proving yourself as a reliable buyer first, but don't underestimate the importance of this option and other referral sources for buying houses.

Curated Real Estate Deals

Investors simply can't look at every property that can be bought. You can't afford to waste time looking at properties that aren't a good fit. So make sure you set filters for property searches and provide referral sources a tight profile of the criteria you are looking for. It will preserve your relationship as you don't have to repeatedly say no. And it will increase the number of matching properties that you get.

Get Help

Today's successful investor must have a web presence. A quality website that attracts visitors and captures leads is essential. You want state-of-the-art, investor-specific sites that not only capture real estate leads but also include lead management tools, to make sure no good deals fall through the cracks. Driving traffic to your site can be automated as well. There are great programs available that help you set up and manage marketing campaigns that keep quality leads coming directly to your site, your email, and your phone.

Finding the right "formula" for your business is a matter of deciding on your targets and the processes you use to take you where you want it to go.

If you are looking to take down several deals a month, or even get into real estate investing full-time, you'll want some help. At a minimum you should consider a remote assistant for prescreening your deals against your criteria. That way you are only spending your precious time looking at that one out of ten or one out of 100 properties that are actually worth making an offer on. This not only means checking the area, price range, and discount, but also verifying values, rental potential, and repairs. Some investors use cookie-cutter criteria and contracts or letters of interest that assistants can send out.

⌂ TAKEAWAYS

- *Revisit your annual income goals. How many deals will you need to do to meet them?*
- *Working backward, and assuming you'll buy only one of every ten properties you look at, how much time and money do you need to invest in deal finding? What sources will you use to find investment properties?*

WHEN YOUR LENDER
TAKES THE EXIT

What happens when the mortgage lender sends you on a detour? Even the best planned trips can run into detours. The GPS is off the mark, surprise construction work pops up, and it all results in delays. On the road to real estate success, one of the biggest roadblocks is funding gone bad. What then?

When Lenders Bail

Unfortunately, real estate lenders do bail on borrowers. Sometimes there are so many contingencies, conditions, and outs in a loan commitment that there really isn't much commitment at all. So why do they do it? As an investor, how can you anticipate that a lender may back out? What do you do if it happens to you?

Why Lenders Bail

Real estate lenders are in the business of making money by making loans. They want to minimize risk, be assured that the numbers work, and most important, they want to be repaid. Here are some of the common things that can derail your loan:

- Finding out the property's value or condition is unacceptable
- The project details (budget issues for bringing the property up to marketable condition)
- Limited lending areas and locales
- Discovering that the borrower can't meet the six C's (see Chapter 12)
- Finding out the loan was priced and quoted incorrectly
- The lender's expectations for profit margins changed, and it is no longer appealing to them
- New regulations limiting lending
- Financial and liquidity challenges
- Attempting to minimize exposure to loss
- Inability to resell the loan in the secondary market
- Discovery of new information after the loan is made

How to Recognize the Signs

Recognizing the signs that your lender is backing away is critical to investors. If you have to resort to Plan B, then it's best to know as soon as possible. Time is always of the essence in real estate, so know your lender's documentation needs.

Build relationships and respond quickly to lenders' requests. Remember, they're not asking for more documentations for fun—they're doing it to satisfy their capital partners and government regulations. If you are working a new lender relationship, keep a keen eye on how responsive the lender is to your requests and/or application. Always *ask* if your loan request fits the lending criteria—not all lenders are a good match. One critical mistake new borrowers make is seeking funding from the wrong type of lender. Better to know right away. Once you've gotten past the initial introductions and groundwork, pay close attention to the lender and how the process is (or isn't) progressing.

Five Signs Your Lender Is Looking for an Exit

1. Claims paperwork has been lost (repeatedly)
2. Adds new loan conditions after you're into the process
3. Has difficult conditions that are impossible to meet
4. Changes the rate, terms, or amount of the loan
5. Ignores you (no response from your loan officer or primary contact)

What to Do

1. **Clarify the issue immediately.** You should have a good contact whom you can trust to give you straight answers. They might not be able to tell you the whole story, but they can definitely tell you if your experience is just standard or if you are facing a major roadblock. It's better to save yourself the time and stress and nail down any issues right away.

2. **Get an extension on your real estate purchase contract.** If your lending source is looking shaky, chances are you've derailed your timeline for closing. You don't want to risk your earnest money deposit, getting sued for nonperformance, or bruising your industry relationships. So request a contract extension and get it signed early. Give yourself plenty of time.

3. **Apply for another loan.** Talk to your other lenders. Explain the scenario. Deliver the whole loan package, complete with all the due diligence and conditions, so that you can expedite your loan application and get an answer fast. And don't bad-mouth the lender who bailed—you'll make yourself look like a difficult borrower.

Preventive Maintenance

I've already pointed out the importance of seeking the right type of lender and being prepared to get a deal closed. Lender relationships are critical, so vet your lenders. Ask for the names and locations of the last five loans they've closed. Get professional referrals. Work only with online sources of pre-vetted, reliable lenders.

 **TAKEAWAYS**

- *What preventive measures should you take when your lending source is looking shaky?*

38

WHEN YOUR REHAB GOES SOUTH

What You Can Do When Your Rehab Takes a Wrong Turn

How can real estate investors turn it around when rehab projects don't go as hoped?

Fix and flip projects don't always go as expected. That's a given. It's what you do when things get off track that makes all the difference in the end. Taking the rhinoceros approach and just charging ahead, oblivious to the financial minefield, is not a strategy. The property investor with an eagle eye for spotting issues early, who has the bigger-picture view, will have the edge in turning potential pitfalls into bigger rewards.

Why Rehabs Go Wrong

Real estate rehabs, like any renovation or building project, can go off in the ditch really fast for a variety of reasons. Sometimes it is simply the result of poor planning and more specifically:

- Forgoing property inspections and thorough due diligence
- Not conducting further testing for mold, meth labs, and Chinese drywall

- Over (or under) rehabbing for current market conditions
- Failing to obtain accurate contractor quotes in advance
- Failing to get good contractors on the job
- Under budgeting (money and time)
- Not budgeting for overages
- Failing to stick to the budget and scope of work
- Taking the DIY approach on items that need a professional

Other rehab issues that can impact newer real estate investors include:

- Falling in love with the wrong property and trying to force it to work
- Paying contractors before they finish their work
- Failing to secure the property during and after rehab
- Ignoring final inspection requirements
- Changes in local property values
- Damage from natural disasters
- Bad contractors who don't alert you to issues or watch your budget

Coping with Over Budget Issues

The impact of all of these issues generally hits you directly in the budget. If your budget gets blown too far out, you may be lucky to get out without heavy losses. Many novice investors have bankrupted themselves by rushing in without education and with no financial reserves to back them up. In these circumstances:

Step 1: Reevaluate the deal and the numbers (where you are, what you can afford).

Step 2: Reestablish priorities.

Step 3: Ensure that you have access to the money you need to complete the deal.

Step 4: Get going fast, and objectively.

Step 5: Document the issues and remedies, and create better systems and rules for next time.

What's most important is getting the property into a livable and salable condition. If you can't do that, things are likely to only get worse. A habitable, salable property still offers you multiple exit and financial options.

Where to Save

Real estate investors who get stuck can find ways to save and still finish the job.

You can save money on:

- Appliances
- Where you shop for materials
- The quality level of materials
- Eliminating low ROI items
- Patching and repairing versus replacing
- Negotiating to pay contractors after you cash out

Where Not to Skimp

Do *not* skimp on your marketing budget!

Your marketing budget is what is going to get the opportunity turned into profit and get cash coming back in. Every day, holding costs are eating into your bottom line to cash out—or, for the buy and hold investor, it means loss of cash flow.

Focus on getting the property into a livable and marketable state while still accounting for all of your expenses and desired profit.

When Investors Need More Money

What if you absolutely need to come up with more cash to finish the project?

Watch these two golden rules:

1. Raise more money as early as you can.
2. Protect your credit so that you don't get cut off from capital.

One of the worst mistakes that new real estate investors make is immediately turning to their savings and personal credit cards to try to finish the project. All too often this results in completely running out of cash and destroying credit ratings to the point of not being able to borrow. Once you are in that place and the property still isn't livable, you may not even be able to afford to file for bankruptcy. Pull in partners—money is attracted to opportunity. If there's an opportunity to make money, partners and funding will follow.

Working with Your Lender When You Need More Money

There is a chance your current lender will provide more cash, but you have to ask. And the earlier, the better. This is especially true of alternative lenders, asset-based lenders, and commercial real estate and specialist rehab lenders. They may be able to "open up" your loan and provide more funds. If you have lender money in escrow to reimburse you for repairs made, you might be able to get that money early, too. Lenders usually don't want to risk losing their capital and will want to work with you, *if* you can show them some better numbers. Go in with a game plan.

Other Capital Sources

Your existing lender may not be able to help and may be very wary about throwing good money after bad. You should be cautious here, too. It may be better to eat the loss, for a clear exit, rather than gambling more money on the unknown.

Before you tap your children's college tuition or the retirement funds or destroy your credit rating:

- Ask other mortgage lenders about a refinance.
- Apply for a different type of loan if the property is in livable condition and value is up.
- Look into home equity loans and lines of credit.
- Check out business loan lenders and business lines of credit.
- Don't overlook friends and family for cash or partnership possibilities.

Four Strategies for Turning Your Rehab Nightmare into Cash

1. Complete your rehab using lower-end finishes and rent it instead of selling it (if your funding is secured for a longer term).
2. Sell it as-is and cash out versus renting it out.
3. Offer the property "designer ready" or have the buyer pay for custom finishes.
4. Try "pre-habbing" or "whole-tailing," a hybrid that's a step up from simple wholesaling but not quite rehabbing for retail sale.

TAKEAWAYS

- *Suppose you have a rehab under way. You take stock of the project and discover that you are $5,000 over budget and at least two weeks behind schedule. What can you do to get your project on track and/or minimize losses?*

39

WHAT IF YOU CAN'T MAKE GOOD ON YOUR INVESTMENT PROPERTY LOAN?

Sometimes real estate investors just can't pay their loans on time. What happens then? What options might be on the table? What happens if you fall into foreclosure?

Why Investors Can't Pay Their Loans

Real estate investors don't generally go into a deal or sign for a loan with the intention of not paying. You've done your numbers and your market research. You've educated yourself and don't see any way this deal can go sideways on you. Sometimes it just does anyway. It may happen rarely, but it's good to be aware of some of the issues that have hit others, so you can avoid them.

These issues include:

- Surprise repairs
- Running over rehab budgets
- Rogue contractors
- Cash flow held up from other deals
- Market changes

- Local weather catastrophes
- Personal financial emergencies
- Nonperforming tenants
- End-buyers who backed out or delayed closings
- Missing insurance or tax payments

Knowing Your Options

If you tackle the issue early, you have options. If you bury your head in the sand and drag your feet, you can guarantee those options are going to dry up and things will only get worse. The earlier you deal with it, the better the outcome is going to be.

Your Options:

- Approach your current lender to get extensions or other options.
- Try pledging equity in other property to get a line of credit.
- Consider a secured line of credit against other assets or savings.
- Ask friends and family for help.
- Bring in a partner on the real estate deal.
- Try to refinance with another investment property lender.
- Check out peer-to-peer lending sites.
- Consider real estate crowdfunding.

Three VIPs:

1. Get new financing closed before you go thirty days late.
2. Take action early.
3. Have a documented plan of how you'll turn around the situation.

What Happens When Investors Don't Pay Their Loans?

If you are simply going to be a few days late in paying your mortgage payment and are 100 percent certain that you won't be more than thirty days late, you probably don't need to stress yourself out or panic. Regardless, call your lender. Stay on top of it. If you are responsive to the situation, your lender is more likely to be responsive as well. If there is a chance you might run over thirty days, you've got to get on your game, fast!

How bad the situation gets, and how fast, may depend on:

- Where you are at in your loan
- The amount of equity you have
- The current condition and status of the property
- The current market
- Who your mortgage lender and loan servicer is

In all cases you can expect your phone to ring off the hook, the mailbox to fill up with notices, and eventually for attorney's letters to come. You may even be served a notice of default (NOD). During this time there will be mounting fees, accrued interest, and fees for attorney's letters. All of this makes it harder to catch up and must be avoided.

If all your efforts to bring the loan current fail, eventually the loan will go into foreclosure. How long a foreclosure will take depends on the laws of the state, current foreclosure volumes, as well as the type of loan. A business or commercial real estate loan can fall into foreclosure in just a few days. Residential real estate loans may take ninety days or more before they get into the court system. Just know that as the market improves foreclosure times are being cut rapidly.

Even though the bank may seize the property as collateral, that doesn't mean that borrowers are off the hook for their debt. Depending on local laws, creditors may still pursue deficiency judgments from borrowers for money owed, even after the property has been forfeited.

Alternatives to Foreclosure

Banks and mortgage lenders usually do not want to foreclose. They are in the money business, not the real estate business. They do not want the situation to get progressively worse and risk losing capital and the money of their investors. However, there may be some cases in which it is more appealing for lenders to foreclose than to cut borrowers a break. So don't assume anything or take for granted the option to work things out.

Options that may be available instead of going through foreclosure may include:

- Loan modifications and recapitalization plans
- Selling the property as-is
- Reinstating the loan
- Short sales
- Signing over the deed in lieu of foreclosure
- Having someone else buy the note and become your new lender

A loan modification that gives you time to pay, without making the terms even harder to keep up with, can be a viable option that creates a fair compromise for both borrower and lender. Expect fees and changed terms—both of which can be a much better alternative than foreclosure.

Effects of Foreclosure on Real Estate Investors

There are both short- and long-term effects of foreclosure on real estate investors. At a minimum, in the short term, it's likely you will be unable to obtain other financing. No other lender, especially a mortgage lender, is going to want to extend you credit if you are in foreclosure or are fresh out of it. That doesn't mean that you can't find ways to invest in real estate and get back on top of your finances, but it is going to make things a lot harder.

In the wake of the crises of the early 2000s and then the over-tightening of loan requirements, it has finally become easier once again for borrowers to get loans after foreclosure and short sales. Often it is just a two- to three-year waiting period. The foreclosure crisis impacted millions of people in America, including many wealthy real estate moguls and celebrities. It will impact your finances for a long time and recovery is possible, but it is best to avoid a full-blown foreclosure at all costs.

Your credit report will be hampered for at least seven to ten years. The cost of not being able to access credit will make everything in life and business more expensive. You'll make less and pay more for everything. If banks or the feds believe you may be involved in a real estate and mortgage fraud scheme, lenders may even blacklist you altogether. Judgments, collections, and tax penalties may also impact earnings until the debt is satisfied.

So, know your options and get to work solving the situation quickly. If you've already been through foreclosure, you can still invest in real estate, but your borrowing options are certain to be more limited and far more expensive.

TAKEAWAYS

- *For any investor facing the inability to repay a loan, what would you recommend as a course of action?*
- *List at least five alternatives and how they can work.*

WHEN THE WHEELS COME OFF YOUR REAL ESTATE INVESTMENT VENTURE

What do you do when you're facing a failure in real estate? Sometimes real estate investment plans fail. In spite of the best hopes and plans, it doesn't always work out as expected. What do you do then?

If there is one thing that we should learn from the most successful real estate and business leaders out there, it is to embrace failures. They are often the catalyst for the greatest successes. So, if your real estate investment doesn't go right, what should you do next?

It Happens to the Best of Us

Millions of Americans "failed" in real estate in the last couple of decades. That includes wealthy celebrities and average citizens. *Shark Tank* investor Barbara Corcoran, who started in real estate with just $1,000 and grew it to a $5 billion empire, says the best thing entrepreneurs can do is embrace failure. In fact, she says it is the most important thing they can do.

You can be smart, rich, and bullish. But that won't guarantee you sustainable success the first time around. If it weren't for great minds and risk takers who were willing to try again, we wouldn't have electricity, the telephone, the internet, mortgage loans, and let's not forget, good vacuum cleaners.

So how can real estate investors minimize the chance of failure? Get back in the saddle after some bumps in the road? How can you make sure things go better in the future? And who is going to work with you even if you've taken a few extreme detours from real estate success in the past?

Why Do Real Estate Investors Fail?

The biggest failure of all is still not trying real estate investment. If you don't try it, you've already failed—guaranteed. From those who have invested in real estate, there are some lessons learned. Some of the most common reasons for failure are:

- Poor budgeting of renovations
- Buying properties with negative cash flow
- Surprise repairs after failing to do due diligence
- Real estate and mortgage fraud
- Borrowing too much
- Rushing in without getting educated first
- Overconfidence
- Ignoring commonsense investment principles

Businesses come and go in any sector and any economy. From a broader perspective, the top reasons for business failures include:

- Emotional pricing
- Operating and living beyond means
- Failure to pay taxes
- Lack of planning
- No knowledge of financing

- Lack of experience in record keeping
- Expanding too fast
- Inadequate and ineffective borrowing practices
- Wasted advertising budget
- Going into business for the wrong reasons

Tips for Preventing Failure in Real Estate Investment

Whether starting out with one investment property or launching a real estate investment business, it is pretty clear the best way to prevent failure is to avoid the pitfalls we've just covered. Do this by:

- Planning thoroughly
- Completing all needed due diligence
- Learning about financing
- Borrowing better, and enough
- Keeping better records
- Staying on top of taxes
- Watching your budgets
- Living within your means
- Having insurance
- Having legal help on call
- Sticking to common sense

Tips for Getting Back on the Road to Real Estate Riches

What if your child fell off a bicycle the first time they tried to ride one? You'd insist they try again, right? You'd think it was crazy if an adult friend of yours told you they have never tried riding a bicycle again after an incident like that, right? So don't even consider not getting back on your journey to building wealth in real estate. It's just a matter of how you do it.

You might want a helmet, some elbow pads, a few tips, and maybe even someone riding alongside you so that you don't crash and burn again. Find a mentor; hire a coach and network with successful investors to learn the lessons of the pros.

- Be objective about past failures (it's not you, it's what you do).
- Analyze what went wrong and what you can do better.
- Invest in learning more about your craft and the real estate market.
- Put safety precautions in place, and avoid the pitfalls.
- Get busy moving forward.

Opportunity Is Knocking

If you've had a deal or a whole portfolio go wrong in the past, don't let it hold you back. This is opportunity knocking, right now. It's waiting for you.

There are lots of great real estate investment opportunities out there. And even with a few battle scars, there are a number of real estate lenders to work with you. Be prepared to talk about what happened and to use the experience to demonstrate that, despite what happened, you know what to do, and what not to do. That's an asset. That's an advantage.

INDEX

THREE FREE RESOURCES
FOR REAL ESTATE INVESTORS

1. FUNDING FOR REAL ESTATE INVESTORS

Need to get a real estate investment funded? CiX.com is where you start.

• Get Funded By Visiting CiX.com •

2. WATCH US REALLY FLIP PROPERTIES

Do you learn better by watching rather than reading? Watch the full docu-series on finding, funding, and flipping investment real estate.

• Binge Watch Season 1 At ReallyFlip.com •

3. BECOME A CONNECTED INVESTOR

Inside Connected Investors you can easily connect with local real estate investors and quickly find deeply discounted investment properties.

• **Join Now. 100% FREE: ConnectedInvestors.com** •